STANDING ON THE EDGE OF ETERNITY

Gary Hamrick

HARVEST HOUSE PUBLISHERS
EUGENE, OREGON

Cover design by Kyler Dougherty
Cover images © ardasavasciogullari, AdobeBox / Getty Images
Interior design by Janelle Coury

For bulk, special sales, or ministry purchases, please call 1-800-547-8979.
Email: CustomerService@hhpbooks.com

STANDING ON THE EDGE OF ETERNITY

Published by Harvest House Publishers
Eugene, Oregon 97408
www.harvesthousepublishers.com

ISBN 978-0-7369-9145-2 (pbk)
ISBN 978-0-7369-9146-9 (eBook)

Library of Congress Control Number: 2024947916

Printed in the United States of America

25 26 27 28 29 30 31 32 33 / BP / 10 9 8 7 6 5 4 3 2 1

To my precious wife, Terri: Thank you for your deep dedication to our Lord and your wonderful support and prayers for me over the years that we have served Jesus together. I love you.

To my wonderful children, Tyler, Austin, and Lindsey: I am grateful to our heavenly Father that He chose me to be your earthly dad. Thank you for loving Jesus and serving Him as you do. I love you.

To my amazing church family, Cornerstone Chapel: What a privilege it is to be your pastor. Thank you for your commitment to knowing the Lord and making Him known! I love you.

May we look forward to the hope of eternity together!

Contents

Foreword—Amir Tsarfati 7

Revelation at 30,000 Feet 9

1. The King in Glory: Revelation 1 19

2. Letters Through the Ages: Revelation 2 33

3. Letters to Our Age: Revelation 3 57

4. The Throne in Heaven: Revelation 4 75

5. Behold, the Lamb: Revelation 5 89

6. The Beginning of the End: Revelation 6 97

7. The Remnant: Revelation 7 109

8. The Calm and the Storm: Revelation 8 121

9. Out of the Abyss: Revelation 9 131

10. A Bittersweet Prophecy: Revelation 10 143

11. A Call to Repentance: Revelation 11 153

12. A Temporary Reign of Terror: Revelation 12 165

13. The Two Beasts: Revelation 13 175

14. Protected from Wrath: Revelation 14 189

15. Rejoicing in Heaven: Revelation 15 201

16. Torment on Earth: Revelation 16 207

17. The Fall of the One-World Religion: Revelation 17 221

18. The Fall of the One-World Government: Revelation 18 . . . 233

19. The Conquering King: Revelation 19 243

20. The Prince of Peace: Revelation 20 261

21. A New Beginning: Revelation 21 283

22. A Glimpse into Eternity: Revelation 22 299

Notes 317

Foreword

AMIR TSARFATI

When I learned that pastor Gary Hamrick wrote a book on Revelation, I was very excited. The message God gave through the apostle John is so important; it's one that more pastors should take the time to walk their congregations through. Gary's approach in *Standing on the Edge of Eternity*—a blend of teaching and commentary—serves as an excellent tool for the common reader. You'll want to have this book next to you as you read through the visions God gave to John about His future plans. If you see a passage or phrase and wonder, *What does that mean?*, chances are pastor Gary provides the answer. And the questions and takeaways for each chapter are wonderful for personal and group study.

Looking at the world around us, it is difficult to deny the signs of the end times. We see an alliance forming between Russia, Iran, Turkey, and other states exactly as we find prophesied in Ezekiel. The once-incomprehensible idea that everyone around the world could watch an event in Jerusalem all at once, or that the global population could be technologically and universally linked through some sort of code or device, now makes perfect sense. And as European alliances are growing ever tighter, a new world leader may arise.

Since the horrific events of October 7, 2023, the people in my country, Israel, have been reeling, experiencing constant ups and downs as our military victories and efforts to defend ourselves are condemned and muted by international outrage. The peace we feel when an air raid siren is silenced becomes a twist in the gut when we remember the Israeli hostages held captive by Hamas, deprived of nourishment, sunlight, civility, and hope. Some were deprived of life entirely.

As a Jewish believer in Yeshua the Messiah, however, I am blessed with the benefit of the big picture. I mourn with my fellow Israelis, but I also recognize that the wars with Iran, Hamas, Hezbollah, the Houthis, and Syria all fit into God's plan. I understand that God is bringing Israel through difficulties now to achieve a place of peace and safety later. This peace is the landscape for the war described in Ezekiel 38 and 39—the war that will open the door for the period known as "Jacob's trouble," described vividly in Revelation.

I often say that I'm not a prophet; I just read my Bible. Pastor Gary can say the same thing. He is a wonderful teacher and a wise student of God's Word. In his book, he quotes Jesus' words in John 14, when the Lord promises that after He has gone to prepare a place for us, He will return so that we can be with Him. It is with pastor Gary's own response to this wonderful promise that I will conclude this foreword:

That is our hope. Jesus is coming again. With joyful expectation, we can and should study the book of Revelation.

Awaiting His return,
Amir Tsarfati

Revelation at 30,000 Feet

Studying Revelation is a bit like drinking out of a fire hose. Whether you are a new Christian, a mature Christian, or not a Christian at all, if you want to understand Revelation, a proper foundation is imperative. Legendary NFL coach Vince Lombardi started each season with his team by holding up a football and announcing the obvious: "Gentlemen, this is a football!" He began with the basics, and so must we. This compilation, based on a series of sermons originally given over multiple months, was created to help you see the signs of the times. You are welcome to follow along with the sermons at *cornerstonechapel.net/teachings*.

A Proper Foundation

To understand the hope and joyful expectation the promise of Jesus Christ's return brings, we must first understand His ascension into heaven. The book of Acts tells us that after Jesus was crucified and buried, He rose from the grave three days later, walked among people for 40 days, and ascended into heaven from the Mount of Olives while His apostles gazed up at Him.

> **Acts 1:1-11**—"The former account I made, O Theophilus, of all that Jesus began both to do and teach, until the day in which He was taken up, after He through the Holy Spirit had given commandments to the apostles whom He had chosen, to whom He also presented Himself alive after His suffering by many infallible proofs, being seen by them during forty days and speaking of the things pertaining to the kingdom of God.
>
> "And being assembled together with them, He commanded them not to depart from Jerusalem, but to wait for the Promise of the Father, 'which,' He said, 'you have heard from Me; for John truly baptized with water, but you shall be baptized with the Holy Spirit not many days from now.' Therefore, when they had come together, they asked Him, saying, 'Lord, will You at this time restore the kingdom to Israel?' And He said to them, 'It is not for you to know times or seasons which the Father has put in His own authority. But you shall receive power when the Holy Spirit has come upon you; and you shall be witnesses to Me in Jerusalem, and in all Judea and Samaria, and to the end of the earth.'
>
> "Now when He had spoken these things, while they watched, He was taken up, and a cloud received Him out of their sight. And while they looked steadfastly toward heaven as He went up, behold, two men stood by them in white apparel, who also said, 'Men of Galilee, why do you stand gazing up into heaven? This same Jesus, who was taken up from you into heaven, will so come in like manner as you saw Him go into heaven.'"

This passage promises that as Jesus departed, so will He return. Although no one knows the day or the time that Jesus will appear, we should learn the signs indicated in Revelation and consider world events through the lens of His imminent return.

> **Matthew 16:1-3**—"The Pharisees and Sadducees came, and testing Him asked that He would show them a sign from

> heaven. He answered and said to them, 'When it is evening you say, "It will be fair weather, for the sky is red"; and in the morning, "It will be foul weather today, for the sky is red and threatening." Hypocrites! You know how to discern the face of the sky, but you cannot discern the signs of the times.'"

Revelation makes for heavy reading—featuring visions of hail, fire, demons, and the Antichrist—yet we do not need to be fearful. God gave us this information in advance so that we can be ready now, like giddy students finding a cheat sheet before taking an exam.

> **John 14:1-3**—"Let not your heart be troubled; you believe in God, believe also in Me. In My Father's house are many mansions; if it were not so, I would have told you. I go to prepare a place for you. And if I go and prepare a place for you, I will come again and receive you to Myself; that where I am, there you may be also."

That is our hope. Jesus is coming again. With joyful expectation, we can and should study the book of Revelation.

Background

The apostle John wrote Revelation by inspiration of the Holy Spirit around AD 95. John, the oldest and last surviving of the 12 apostles, was likely in his nineties when he wrote from a prison camp on a little island in the Aegean Sea, called Patmos. The Roman Emperor Domitian persecuted Christians who would not denounce their faith, including John, whom he had banished to the Roman labor camp on Patmos. Yet the Lord had greater plans for John and gave him an incredible revelation while he was there.

Notice this is the revelation of Jesus Christ, not the revelation of John. The word "Revelation" in the Greek text of Revelation 1:1 is *apokalupsis*, which is where we get our English word *apocalypse*. It means "an unveiling" or "a revealing." This book is a revelation of the Son of God. John was simply the instrument whom God used to communicate the revelation of Jesus Christ.

Methods of Interpretation

Proper interpretation is critical to proper understanding. There are three major methods people use when they interpret Revelation: allegorical, historical, and literal or futuristic.

Allegorical—The allegorical method views all of Revelation as symbolism: good versus evil, paganism versus Christianity, and the ultimate triumph of Christ in the lives of believers. This view sees Revelation as a spiritual allegory for the comfort and encouragement of the church, and denies that the book presents prophecies of literal, future events.

Historical—There are two historical views:

> *Preterist view.* According to this view, Revelation describes church history, specifically the early church's struggle against Imperial Rome, with John using symbolic code to recount the events of his day. It shares similarities with the allegorical method, representing certain elements of Revelation as symbolic rather than prophetic.
>
> *Total view.* In this perspective, Revelation describes all of church history from the Roman Empire until today, culminating in the second coming. Those who subscribe to the total view think Revelation is a symbolic interpretation of the church's struggle against the world system.

Both the allegorical and historical views consider Revelation as a symbolic representation of historical events rather than a prophecy of what is to come.

Literal or Futuristic—In the literal/futuristic view, Revelation is prophetic. Therefore, John speaks prophetically of literal, future events beginning in Revelation 4:1. Symbolism is frequently present, but events unfold in a literal way. Among those who hold to this view, there are differences of opinion regarding the timing of the rapture of the church.

The literal/futuristic view is how I interpret Revelation and is the lens through which we will study the book.

An Outline

> **REVELATION 1:19**–"Write the things which you have seen, and the things which are, and the things which will take place after this."

Jesus' command to John provides an outline for the entire book of Revelation:

1. Write the things which you have seen. In chapter 1, John wrote about the majestic vision that Jesus gave him.
2. Write about the things which are. In chapters 2–3, John wrote seven letters to seven different literal churches, which signify the church age.
3. Write about the things which will take place after this. In chapters 4–22, John wrote about future events.

The Church Age

The church age began when Jesus ascended into heaven and continues to this day. Believers are entrusted with the sacred privilege of sharing the good news of the gospel so that as many people as possible might come to faith in Christ.

We do not know how long the church age is going to last, but it will end with the rapture of the church alluded to in Revelation 4. The Bible says there will be a generation of believers who will be physically snatched from the earth and taken up to be with the Lord.

The Second Coming

The second coming of Christ will happen in two phases:

Phase One—Jesus alone will come down in the clouds and sound a trumpet call. The dead in Christ will rise first. Their spirits are already in heaven, but during phase one, their bodies will play catch-up and become glorified. Then those believers who are alive and remain on the earth will be called up together with them to receive their glorified bodies and meet the Lord in the air.

Paul describes this first phase in 1 Thessalonians:

> **1 Thessalonians 4:16-17**—"The Lord Himself will descend from heaven with a shout, with the voice of an archangel, and with the trumpet of God. And the dead in Christ will rise first. Then we who are alive and remain shall be caught up together with them in the clouds to meet the Lord in the air. And thus we shall always be with the Lord."

"Caught up" in the Greek text is *harpazō*, but in the Latin Vulgate, which is the Latin translation of the Bible, it is *raptus*. *Raptus* is where we get our English word *rapture*.

When the rapture happens, there will be an entire generation of believers who will not experience death! Imagine going up—no funeral for you! Those who are alive at the time of Christ's return will be given their glorified bodies on the way up to heaven:

> **1 Corinthians 15:51-52**—"Behold, I tell you a mystery: We shall not all sleep, but we shall all be changed—in a moment, in the twinkling of an eye, at the last trumpet. For the trumpet will sound, and the dead will be raised incorruptible, and we shall be changed."

Following phase one will come seven years of tribulation on the earth (Revelation 6–18). Scripture does not specify how soon after the rapture the tribulation will begin, but Christians will be gone from the earth and cataclysmic events will occur. There will be meteor showers, 100-pound hailstones, fresh water turned to blood, famine, diseases, and boils. Many will die.

As a loving Father, this will be God's final attempt to get people's attention and prevent the loss of their souls to hell. They do not have to die and stay eternally separated from God. They end up in hell when they stubbornly refuse to believe in the Lord.

Phase Two—After the seven years of tribulation, the Lord Jesus will return to the same place from which He ascended on the Mount of Olives, and the saints who were kept safe in heaven will return with Him for the battle of Armageddon.

Following His victory at Armageddon, Jesus will usher in 1,000 years during which He will rule and reign on the earth (Revelation 20). This period is known as the millennium. At the end of that time, there will be a great judgment in which Satan will be thrown into the lake of fire. At this great white throne judgment, unbelievers will have to stand before the throne and give account of their lives.

Finally, Revelation 21 and 22 describe a new heaven and a new earth because the present heaven and earth will be destroyed. Do not take this the wrong way, environmentalists, but this world is going to burn! In his second epistle, Peter gives us a glimpse of that day:

> **2 Peter 3:10-13**—"The day of the Lord will come as a thief in the night, in which the heavens will pass away with a great noise, and the elements will melt with fervent heat; both the earth and the works that are in it will be burned up. Therefore, since all these things will be dissolved, what manner of persons ought you to be in holy conduct and godliness, looking for and hastening the coming of the day of God, because of which the heavens will be dissolved, being on fire, and the elements will melt with fervent heat? Nevertheless we, according to His promise, look for new heavens and a new earth in which righteousness dwells."

John's Descriptions

Unfamiliar Sights—Imagine if George Washington were to see a flat-screen television or a cell phone. How would he describe such an object in a time without plastic or electricity? When we read Revelation, we must consider that John used descriptions relevant to his own time to speak of a time to come.

John's senses were bombarded by visions and sounds wholly unfamiliar to him. His descriptions about the future appear to be mystical because he had limited language with which to describe these events.

A Polychronic View—We must also realize that Westerners generally think chronologically. At times, John wrote Revelation with a polychronic or circular view, a view common in Eastern countries that focuses less on linear time and more on multiple events happening at once.

To understand this circular view, imagine John standing in a circular room. On the wall all around him are televisions projecting different images. He writes as he sees all these different things happening in the room around him.

Not Everyone Is the Antichrist

Some people tend to read Revelation and assume that everything we see in our world today is a prophetic fulfillment of this book. But here are some examples of why we should avoid reading our present circumstances into Revelation, particularly in relation to identifying the Antichrist:

Ronald Reagan

In the 1980s, some people believed that President Ronald Reagan was the Antichrist because each of the three names in Ronald Wilson Reagan included six letters. They determined that this was representative of the mark of the beast, or the Antichrist, which Revelation 13:18 says is "666."

Adolf Hitler

In the 1930s, some in the church were convinced that Hitler was the Antichrist and Joseph Stalin was the False Prophet. As Panzer tanks pulled up to churches throughout Europe, church leaders assured Christians that they would be raptured. Yet the rapture did not happen. Ten thousand pastors were killed during World War II for refusing to bow to Nazi Germany. The church became disillusioned, wondering why Jesus had not returned to take them home.

Barcodes and Chips

Later, barcodes and credit card chips were considered the mark of the beast. But we cannot be so convinced of our own ideas that our faith is lost if things do not happen as we expect. Yet there are warning signs, "birth pains" (Matthew 24:8 NIV), we should be cognizant of. Our world is falling apart, but Jesus is Lord of all. He will come again and take us home to be with Him. We must be ready with joyful anticipation of His imminent return. Our redemption draws near.

1

The King in Glory

REVELATION 1

The book of Revelation talks about judgment, death, and the Antichrist, and while those are all fearsome things, Revelation is a book of hope. Remember, Revelation was written amid tribulation. When John received this vision, he was in exile for the sake of the gospel, sent to the island of Patmos to slave away in his old age. But amid this darkness, Jesus brought light. This is a prominent theme throughout the book: Jesus is the light amid the darkness, and He promises a blessing on those who read and "hear the words of this prophecy" (Revelation 1:3). So let us look forward to Jesus' return with hope.

> **REVELATION 1:1-3**—"The Revelation of Jesus Christ, which God gave Him to show His servants—things which must shortly take place. And He sent and signified it by His angel to His servant John, who bore witness to the word of God, and to the testimony of Jesus Christ, to all things that he saw. Blessed is he who reads and those who hear the words of this prophecy, and keep those things which are written in it; for the time is near."

Shortly Take Place

John was not suggesting that the events in Revelation would necessarily happen soon. "Shortly take place" is *en tachei* in the Greek text, which translates to "quickly" or "suddenly." John was communicating that when the events in Revelation do occur, they will happen suddenly.

Angels

There are 76 mentions of angels in Revelation. God used angels to assist with delivering visions to John:

> **Revelation 5:2**—"I saw a strong angel proclaiming with a loud voice, 'Who is worthy to open the scroll and to loose its seals?'"
>
> **Revelation 7:2a**—"I saw another angel ascending from the east, having the seal of the living God."

A Circular View

Revelation discusses things John "saw" 36 times, and things John "heard" 27 times. As mentioned earlier, while much of Revelation is chronological, as an Easterner, John sometimes described his visions in a polychronic, circular fashion.

A Prophetic Writing

Although some people do not view Revelation as prophecy, John said it plainly in Revelation 1:3: "Blessed is he who reads and those who hear the words of this prophecy."

The Beatitudes of Revelation

"Blessed" in the Greek text translates to "oh, how happy," and *beatitude* means "supreme blessedness." There are seven beatitudes in Revelation:

> **Revelation 1:3a**—"Blessed is he who reads and those who hear the words of this prophecy."

Revelation 14:13b—"Blessed are the dead who die in the Lord from now on."

Revelation 16:15b—"Blessed is he who watches."

Revelation 19:9b—"Blessed are those who are called to the marriage supper of the Lamb!"

Revelation 20:6a—"Blessed and holy is he who has part in the first resurrection."

Revelation 22:7b—"Blessed is he who keeps the words of the prophecy of this book."

Revelation 22:14—"Blessed are those who do His commandments, that they may have the right to the tree of life, and may enter through the gates into the city."

Revelation begins and ends with blessing!

REVELATION 1:4-6—"John, to the seven churches which are in Asia:

> "Grace to you and peace from Him who is and who was and who is to come, and from the seven Spirits who are before His throne, and from Jesus Christ, the faithful witness, the firstborn from the dead, and the ruler over the kings of the earth.
>
> "To Him who loved us and washed us from our sins in His own blood, and has made us kings and priests to His God and Father, to Him be glory and dominion forever and ever. Amen."

Seven Churches

"Asia" is specifically in reference to Asia Minor, which is in modern-day Turkey. Jesus dictated seven letters to the seven pastors of the seven churches in Asia Minor, while John recorded them on Jesus' behalf in Revelation chapters 2 and 3.

While the churches were literal, they each also represented a specific time in church history leading up to Christ's second coming, and God had a specific message for each literal church and each period of church history.

Seven Spirits

There are three perspectives regarding the identity of the "seven Spirits who are before His throne."

1. Fullness of the Spirit

The number seven is mentioned more than 50 times in Revelation. Throughout Scripture, the number seven represents things that are perfect or complete, so some scholars believe that the "seven Spirits" represent the fullness of the Holy Spirit.

2. Seven Virtues of the Spirit

> **Isaiah 11:2**—"The Spirit of the Lord shall rest upon Him, the Spirit of wisdom and understanding, the Spirit of counsel and might, the Spirit of knowledge and of the fear of the Lord."

Isaiah prophesied those words about Jesus, describing the seven characteristics of the Holy Spirit who would "rest upon Him." Some scholars believe the term "seven Spirits" references those virtues.

3. Seven Angels

Scholars who adopt this position believe the seven Spirits before God's throne in Revelation 1:4 are the seven angels before God's throne described in Revelation 8:2—"I saw the seven angels who stand before God, and to them were given seven trumpets."

This is the interpretation I believe makes the most sense.

Firstborn from the Dead

Jesus Christ was the first person to rise from the dead in a glorified body. Scripture offers instances where God chose to raise individuals from the dead, such as Jesus' friend Lazarus—but in every case, the person would continue to age and eventually die a second time. Jesus is the only person to rise from the dead in a new, immortal body, never to perish again.

Kings and Priests

When people accept Jesus as their Savior, they become co-heirs with Christ (Romans 8:17). They become priests in the sense that they are now endowed with the responsibility of making God known to man by sharing God's truth with others, and making man known to God by praying for people and interceding for them with the Lord.

> **1 Peter 2:9**—"You are a chosen generation, a royal priesthood, a holy nation, His own special people, that you may proclaim the praises of Him who called you out of darkness into His marvelous light."

What a royal welcome!

> **REVELATION 1:7-8**—"Behold, He is coming with clouds, and every eye will see Him, even they who pierced Him. And all the tribes of the earth will mourn because of Him. Even so, Amen. 'I am the Alpha and the Omega, the Beginning and the End,' says the Lord, 'who is and who was and who is to come, the Almighty.'"

Coming with Clouds

The idea that Jesus will come "with clouds" may be both a literal statement and a figurative one. Here, John was referring to Jesus' second coming to Earth, after the rapture has already occurred.

Jesus will come as He left, physically arriving in the clouds, though the preposition here is "with," not "in."

But Hebrews 11 suggests that rather than just the physical clouds, the "clouds" in Revelation 1:7 can refer to the saints, who will return with Jesus to rule and reign with Him for 1,000 years. Hebrews 11 is known as the "Hall of Faith" and mentions many of the saints whose experiences are recorded in Scripture. Hebrews refers to these saints as "a cloud of witnesses."

> **Hebrews 12:1**—"Therefore we also, since we are surrounded by so great a cloud of witnesses, let us lay aside every weight, and the sin which so easily ensnares us, and let us run with endurance the race that is set before us."

The book of Matthew describes Jesus' return to Earth as "on the clouds."

> **Matthew 26:64**—"Jesus said to him, 'It is as you said. Nevertheless, I say to you, hereafter you will see the Son of Man sitting at the right hand of the Power, and coming on the clouds of heaven.'"

However, the preposition "on" can also be interpreted to mean "in" or "with" the clouds. In fact, in Revelation, this preposition changes to "with."

> **Revelation 1:7**—"Behold, He is coming with clouds, and every eye will see Him, even they who pierced Him. And all the tribes of the earth will mourn because of Him. Even so, Amen."

And 1 Thessalonians also uses "with" to describe that Jesus is coming alongside His saints:

> **1 Thessalonians 3:12-13 (ESV)**—"May the Lord make you increase and abound in love for one another and for all, as we do for you, so that he may establish your hearts blameless in holiness before our God and Father, at the coming of our Lord Jesus with all his saints."

Old Testament References

The Old Testament is referenced more than 300 times in Revelation, although most instances are not cross-referenced. The description of Jesus given in Revelation 1:7-8 was also presented by the prophet Daniel:

> **Daniel 7:13-14**—"I was watching in the night visions, and behold, One like the Son of Man, coming with the clouds of heaven! He came to the Ancient of Days, and they brought Him near before Him. Then to Him was given dominion and glory and a kingdom, that all peoples, nations, and languages should serve Him. His dominion is an everlasting dominion, which shall not pass away, and His kingdom the one which shall not be destroyed."

Every Eye Will See Him

The second coming of Christ will not happen in obscurity. Although Jesus will return to the Mount of Olives, all will be able to see Him. Possibly, advanced technology will accomplish this.

The Jewish People Weep

The sins of all people nailed Jesus to the cross, but the phrase "even they who pierced Him" is a special notation for the Jewish people.

> **Zechariah 12:10-11**—"I will pour on the house of David and on the inhabitants of Jerusalem the Spirit of grace and supplication; then they will look on Me whom they pierced. Yes, they will mourn for Him as one mourns for his only son, and grieve for Him as one grieves for a firstborn. In that day there shall be a great mourning in Jerusalem, like the mourning at Hadad Rimmon in the plain of Megiddo."

When Jesus finally appears on the earth, the Jewish people will weep bitterly, as will all who denied Him. People will be undone at the sight of the Lord.

All the Tribes of the Earth

Revelation 7:9 describes "all nations, tribes, peoples, and tongues, standing before the throne." Heaven will be diverse. Jesus came for all, died for all, and loves all.

The Sum of Everything

God is described as the "Almighty" ten times in the New Testament, and nine of those instances are in Revelation. He is also called the "Alpha and Omega," which references the first and last letters of the Greek alphabet. This translates to *Aleph Tav* in Hebrew and means "the sum total of everything."

> **REVELATION 1:9-11**—"I, John, both your brother and companion in the tribulation and kingdom and patience of Jesus Christ, was on the island that is called Patmos for the word of God and for the testimony of Jesus Christ. I was in the Spirit on the Lord's Day, and I heard behind me a loud voice, as of a trumpet, saying, 'I am the Alpha and the Omega, the First and the Last,' and, 'What you see, write in a book and send it to the seven churches which are in Asia: to Ephesus, to Smyrna, to Pergamos, to Thyatira, to Sardis, to Philadelphia, and to Laodicea.'"

Tribulation and Persecution

When John used the word "tribulation" in verse 9, he was not referencing the seven years of tribulation discussed later in Revelation, but rather, the tribulations and persecution Christians endured in the first century. Remember, his punishment on Patmos was a result of his faithfulness to "the word of God and for the testimony of Jesus Christ." He refused to renounce Christ and faced tribulation as a result.

Captive by the Spirit

The article "the" was not present in the original Greek text, so the literal translation for verse 10 is "I was in Spirit." This communicates that John experienced something more than the presence of the Holy Spirit. Rather, John was captive by, or caught up in, the Holy Spirit, and God supernaturally transported him somewhere to see this incredible vision.

Jesus Speaking

The voice John heard was that of Jesus Himself, who gave John a command to write down the visions he saw. Eleven more times, Jesus would remind John to write. John may have been so awestruck over the things that he saw that Jesus had to continually redirect him.

> **REVELATION 1:12-16**—"I turned to see the voice that spoke with me. And having turned I saw seven golden lampstands, and in the midst of the seven lampstands One like the Son of Man, clothed with a garment down to the feet and girded about the chest with a golden band. His head and hair were white like wool, as white as snow, and His eyes like a flame of fire; His feet were like fine brass, as if refined in a furnace, and His voice as the sound of many waters; He had in His right hand seven stars, out of His mouth went a sharp two-edged sword, and His countenance was like the sun shining in its strength."

Seven Lampstands

The "lampstands" here are a Jewish menorah: a golden, seven-branched candelabra that was used to illuminate the temple. The menorah is a source of light, and the church is to be the light of the world. Hence, the seven lampstands represent the seven specific churches that Jesus would address in chapters 2 and 3.

The Son of Man

The term "Son of Man" is a messianic title applied exclusively to Jesus. Here, John described a vision of Jesus in full glory, with hair like snow, eyes like fire, feet like brass, and a voice like "many waters," representing Jesus' majesty, purity, authority, and glory. When John stated that "out of His mouth went a sharp two-edged sword," he was referencing the Word of God.

John described Jesus in similar terms later in Revelation when discussing Jesus' return to Earth:

> **REVELATION 19:11-16**—"Now I saw heaven opened, and behold, a white horse. And He who sat on him was called Faithful and True, and in righteousness He judges and makes war. His eyes were like a flame of fire, and on His head were many crowns. He had a name written that no one knew except Himself. He was clothed with a robe dipped in blood, and His name is called The Word of God. And the armies in heaven, clothed in fine linen, white and clean, followed Him on white horses. Now out of His mouth goes a sharp sword, that with it He should strike the nations. And He Himself will rule them with a rod of iron. He Himself treads the winepress of the fierceness and wrath of Almighty God. And He has on His robe and on His thigh a name written:
>
> "KING OF KINGS AND LORD OF LORDS."

Jesus is not coming again meek and mild. In His second visit, He is coming as the King of kings.

> **REVELATION 1:17-20**—"When I saw Him, I fell at His feet as dead. But He laid His right hand on me, saying to me, 'Do not be afraid; I am the First and the Last. I am He who lives, and was dead, and behold, I am alive forevermore. Amen. And I have the keys of Hades and of Death. Write the things which you

> have seen, and the things which are, and the things which will take place after this. The mystery of the seven stars which you saw in My right hand, and the seven golden lampstands: The seven stars are the angels of the seven churches, and the seven lampstands which you saw are the seven churches.'"

A Risen Savior

John fell on his face at the sight of his Savior, but Jesus encouraged him to "not be afraid," and reminded John that He conquered sin and death for those who believe by rising from the grave. See, Christianity is the only religion that worships a risen Savior. Gandhi, Confucius, Muhammad, and Buddha are all dead, but Jesus is alive!

An Outline

Once again, in verse 19, Jesus provided an outline for the entire book of Revelation:

1. Write the things which you have seen (*past*). In chapter 1, John wrote about the majestic vision Jesus gave him.
2. Write about the things which are (*present*). John was living in a time known as the church age, and in chapters 2 and 3, he wrote seven letters to seven different literal churches.
3. Write about the things which will take place after this (*future*). In chapters 4–22, John wrote about future events.

Stars and Lampstands

Chapter 1 concludes with Jesus defining the seven lampstands as the seven churches, and the "seven stars" as "the angels of the seven churches."

In this instance, the term "angels" does not refer to the spirit beings that attend to the Lord and circulate in the spirit realm. Rather, the word, in the original Greek text, is *aggelos*, which translates to "messenger," referring to the human vessels God spoke to and who spoke on His behalf. In fact, *aggelos* is the same Greek word Jesus used to describe John the Baptist when He called him "My messenger" in Matthew 11:10.

Jesus never dictated a letter to an angel. He dictated letters to messengers, and the messenger of a church is the pastor. Jesus was talking to the pastors of the seven churches, which were in Ephesus, Smyrna, Pergamos, Thyatira, Sardis, Philadelphia, and Laodicea.

Reflections on Revelation 1

Getting Started

What is the dominant theme of Revelation? Why do you think it is so important for us to keep this in mind as we read the book?

Study Questions

1. How should we understand the phrase "shortly take place" (Revelation 1:1)? Why should this phrase and Jesus' words that "of that day and hour no one knows" (Matthew 24:36) motivate us to godly living?
2. The book of Revelation is peppered with God's blessings. What promise is made in Revelation 1:3? What other blessings are found in Revelation's seven beatitudes?
3. Jesus is described as "the firstborn from the dead" (Colossians 1:18). What promise for the believer is wrapped up in this name of God?
4. What responsibility comes with God calling His people "kings and priests" (Revelation 1:6)? In what practical ways can we live out this calling?
5. What does Hebrews 11 and 12:1 suggest are the "clouds" described in Revelation 1:7?
6. What does the title "Alpha and Omega" (Revelation 1:8, 11) tell you about Jesus? How might this description bring comfort in your Christian walk?
7. What "tribulation" was John referring to in Revelation 1:9? How did John respond to his tribulation, and how should we likewise respond to ours?
8. In Revelation 1:12, the church is symbolized by a Jewish

menorah. Describe the significance of this symbol in relation to the role of the church in the world.

9. Compare Luke 2:4-7 with Revelation 19:11-16. How will Jesus' second coming differ from His first coming?
10. What does Jesus provide for us in Revelation 1:19?

Important Takeaways for Us Today

1. Why should we study what God said to seven churches that no longer physically exist?
2. Read Revelation 1:17-18. What does this passage tell us about the Jesus we serve now? Why is it vital for us to view Jesus not only as the Suffering Servant, but as the King of kings?

2

Letters Through the Ages

REVELATION 2

As we begin reading about the seven churches, we can be tempted to believe the churches were only literal or only symbolic, but the truth is they were both. These churches were seven literal churches located in modern-day Turkey, and they also serve as seven symbols of spiritual truths and historical church periods. So, let us move forward with a balanced view, studying these churches from the time of the apostles into today.

The Seven Letters

A Literal Interpretation

Each church was in what is now modern-day Turkey, south of the Black Sea, and each should be interpreted as the literal church it was. But besides possessing literal context, each church also has a spiritual and historical context.

When we look at a map, we see that Jesus addressed these churches in a clockwise pattern.

Seven Letter Elements

The seven letters to the seven churches address different concerns and offer different advice based on the needs of each one. But despite these differences, the letters all share seven similarities:

1. A greeting addressed to the "angel," or pastor, of their church
2. A special title for Jesus, the author
3. A reminder that Jesus knows their "works" or "deeds"
4. A commendation, complaint, or both
5. An allusion to Jesus' second coming
6. A challenge
7. A reward or promise to the overcomers

Church at Ephesus

Symbolically, Ephesus represents the first-century church from AD 33 to 100. This is the apostolic age, covering from the time of Pentecost to the time when John, the last surviving apostle, died.

History of Ephesus

Ephesus is located on the eastern shore of the Aegean Sea and once had a population of 300,000–500,000 people. Today, a small Turkish village exists there, called Selçuk.

But back in the first century, Ephesus was a prosperous trade-port city given over to the worship of Diana, called Artemis by the Romans, the goddess of sex and fertility. The city was known for immorality. At any one time, this temple had 1,000 prostitutes in it.

Yet amid this pagan society, the light of Christ shone. In the first century AD, Luke recorded in the book of Acts that many Ephesians were getting saved under Paul's ministry and delivered from their occult practices:

> **Acts 19:11-20**—People were saved and burned their books on sorcery, a collection that would be worth around $7 million today.

Acts 19:21-41—When Paul preached the gospel, people began turning to Christ and no longer wanted to purchase man-made idols. The traders of these idols wanted to kill Paul because the rise of Christianity was costing them money.

Letter to Ephesus

1. The Greeting: Directed to the angel, or the pastor, of the church of Ephesus.

REVELATION 2:1a–"To the angel of the church of Ephesus write..."

2. The Title for Jesus: Jesus, who walks amid the seven churches.

REVELATION 2:1b–"He who holds the seven stars in His right hand, who walks in the midst of the seven golden lampstands..."

3. The Reminder:

REVELATION 2:2a–"I know your works."

4. The Commendation: Jesus commended the believers in Ephesus for their perseverance and their discernment. First, He commended their perseverance:

REVELATION 2:3–"You have persevered and have patience, and have labored for My name's sake and have not become weary."

Then Jesus commended them for accurately discerning what is false doctrine—in particular, the false doctrine of the Nicolaitans.

> **REVELATION 2:6**—"You hate the deeds of the Nicolaitans, which I also hate."

The Nicolaitans

This false doctrine is rooted in the Greek understanding of the word "Nicolaitans." This term comes from the words *nikaó*, meaning "to conquer," and *laos*, meaning "the laity." Together, this loosely means "to conquer the laity."

The deeds of the Nicolaitans involved reducing the freedom of the believer to a hierarchical system of priest and laity, whereby one group lorded authority over another group, where a priestly system put a human being between God and man instead of recognizing Jesus as the only mediator between God and man (1 Timothy 2:5).

5. The Complaint: They had left their first love, Jesus.

> **REVELATION 2:4**—"Nevertheless I have this against you, that you have left your first love."

They did not lose their first love—they had left Him. This was an act of human will. A relationship with Jesus cannot be forced. Jesus wants a reciprocal relationship, and so He offers us free will. Thus, we cannot lose our salvation. But there can be a willful rejection of Christ.

6. The Challenge: Listen.

> **REVELATION 2:7a**—"He who has an ear, let him hear what the Spirit says to the churches."

7. The Reward: Eating from the tree of life.

REVELATION 2:7b–"To him who overcomes I will give to eat from the tree of life, which is in the midst of the Paradise of God."

The last time God mentioned the tree of life was back in Genesis 2 and 3, when He guarded the tree from man after Adam and Eve ate from the tree of the knowledge of good and evil, lest man eat it and remain stuck in a fallen state:

> **Genesis 3:22**—"The LORD God said, 'Behold, the man has become like one of Us, to know good and evil. And now, lest he put out his hand and take also of the tree of life, and eat, and live forever.'"

God mentions the tree of life again in Revelation:

> **Revelation 22:2**—"In the middle of its street, and on either side of the river, was the tree of life, which bore twelve fruits, each tree yielding its fruit every month. The leaves of the tree were for the healing of the nations."

Church at Smyrna

Symbolically, Smyrna represents the suffering church from AD 100 to 312. This is the persecuted church, and it covered the period from the end of the apostolic age to when Constantine made Christianity legal in the Roman Empire.

History of Smyrna

Smyrna was located in what is present-day Izmir, Turkey, and now holds a population of about 250,000 people. This city's wealth was second only to Ephesus. Smyrna was along a major trade route from Persia to Rome, a seaport city that traded in a precious commodity known as myrrh.

Myrrh is a gum resin derived from an indigenous shrub. Here are its three uses:

1. As an ingredient in perfume, fragrant only after being crushed (Psalm 45:8)
2. As an ingredient for anointing oil during priestly service (Exodus 30:23)
3. As an element in embalming the dead (John 19:39)

The first use of myrrh as a perfume also has a symbolic meaning in relation to the church at Smyrna, as both were fragrant when crushed. And the believers in the church at Smyrna indeed suffered a great deal.

Suffering Church

The most famous Christian to be martyred in Smyrna was Polycarp, the bishop of Smyrna, who was burned at the stake in his nineties. In bold defiance, Polycarp said, "For over eighty years I have served my Lord and Savior Jesus Christ. Not once has He done me wrong, and I will not blaspheme Him." And he was not alone. Countless Christians were martyred for their faith during this time.

The Christian sign of the fish helped believers secretly identify each other for fear of persecution under the Roman Empire. But when the Romans became aware of this symbol, believers began using the Greek word for fish, *ixthus,* as an acronym for the phrase Jesus Christ, God's Son, Savior. In Greek, the phrase is *Ἰησοῦς Χριστός, Θεοῦ Υἱός, Σωτήρ*, and the first letter of each word spells *ΙΧΘΥΣ*, which happens to be the Greek word for fish.

Letter to Smyrna

1. The Greeting: Directed to the angel, or the pastor, of the church of Smyrna.

> **REVELATION 2:8a**—"To the angel of the church in Smyrna write..."

2. The Title for Jesus:

> **REVELATION 2:8b**—"The First and the Last, who was dead, and came to life..."

This focus on Christ as the resurrection and the life may have been intended to comfort the saints in their present tribulation because many of their friends had been martyred.

3. The Reminder:

> **REVELATION 2:9a**—"I know your works."

4. The Commendation: The saints at Smyrna remained faithful, and this made them rich in the Lord despite their destitution and affliction (Revelation 2:9a). The Bible refers to several spiritual riches God offers His children:

    Romans 2:4—The riches of God's kindness

    Romans 9:23—The riches of God's glory

    Romans 11:33—The riches of God's wisdom and knowledge

    Ephesians 1:7—The riches of God's grace

    Ephesians 1:18—The riches of our glorious inheritance

    Ephesians 3:8—The unsearchable riches of Christ

The Heresy

Jesus then referred to the Judaizers, a group of Jews who believed in adding good works to the simplicity of the gospel by faith in Him, corrupting God's truth from a grace-oriented salvation to a works-oriented message, and the Lord was not pleased with them.

> **REVELATION 2:9b**—"I know the blasphemy of those who say they are Jews and are not, but are a synagogue of Satan."

God called this unbiblical addition "of Satan" because heresies are born of Satan's desire to confound the simplicity of the gospel.

Ten Days

Jesus also noted that the saints at Smyrna would continue to suffer tribulation for "ten days" (Revelation 2:10), which some Bible scholars believe covertly refers to the ten worst Roman emperors:

- Nero, who from AD 64–68 burned Rome and blamed Christians; crucified believers and threw them into pits to be torn apart by wild beasts; executed Paul and Peter; and dipped Christians in tar and turned them into human torches.
- Domitian, who from AD 90–96 killed thousands in Rome and banished the apostle John to slavery on the island of Patmos.
- Trajan, who from AD 104–117 outlawed Christianity and burned Ignatius at the stake.
- Marcus Aurelius, who from AD 161–180 tortured and beheaded Christians, and killed Justin Martyr.
- Septimius Severus, who from AD 200–211 burned, crucified, and beheaded Christians. He also killed Irenaeus.
- Maximinus, who from AD 235–237 executed Christians.
- Decius, who from AD 250–253 tried to wipe out Christianity and killed Alexander of Jerusalem.
- Valerian, who from AD 257–260 tried to eradicate Christianity and executed the bishop of Carthage.
- Aurelian, who from AD 270–275 persecuted Christians any way he could.
- Diocletian, who from AD 303–312 burned the Scriptures,

destroyed churches, and required everyone to offer sacrifices to Roman gods.

5. The Complaint: Smyrna was one of two churches that did not receive a rebuke from Jesus because instead of getting into trouble, the believers were busy suffering for Jesus and doing His work.
6. The Challenge: Listen.

> **REVELATION 2:11a**–"He who has an ear, let him hear what the Spirit says to the churches."

7. The Reward: Jesus made two promises to the faithful.

First, Jesus promised the faithful a crown of life.

> **REVELATION 2:10b**–"Be faithful until death, and I will give you the crown of life."

This verse references one of the five crowns believers can earn before laying them at Jesus' feet someday in heaven:

- The crown of life (Revelation 2:10; James 1:12)
- The incorruptible crown (1 Corinthians 9:25)
- The crown of rejoicing (1 Thessalonians 2:19)
- The crown of righteousness (2 Timothy 4:8)
- The crown of glory (1 Peter 5:4)

Second, Jesus promised the faithful immunity from the second death, a death only for those who were never born again.

> **REVELATION 2:11b**–"He who overcomes shall not be hurt by the second death."

The second death is the lake of fire (eternal death), which follows the first death (natural death):

> **Revelation 20:14-15**—"Then Death and Hades were cast into the lake of fire. This is the second death. And anyone not found written in the Book of Life was cast into the lake of fire."

Church at Pergamos

Chronologically, Pergamos represents the state church from AD 312 to 606. This runs from the time Constantine legalized Christianity, thus making the church vulnerable to Roman pagan customs and practices, to the time when the Roman Catholic Church arose.

History of Pergamos

Pergamos was located 20 miles inland from the Aegean Sea, on the bank of a river about 50 miles north of Smyrna. Now the area is called Bergama and has a population of about 14,000. In the first century, Pergamos was a wealthy city. This is because when an Egyptian pharaoh outlawed the export of papyrus, Eumenes II, the king of Pergamos, got creative and discovered that you could make paper from wood pulp. Paper became one of Pergamos's greatest commodities and was a major source of its wealth. No wonder Pergamos was proud.

The city was filled with people who were arrogant, self-centered, and obsessed with the pursuit of knowledge through books. In fact, with more than 200,000 volumes, the library in Pergamos was one of the largest in its day. Later, those books were taken by Roman general Mark Antony and gifted to Cleopatra, who reigned in Egypt.

And like the cities in the rest of the Roman Empire, Pergamos was polytheistic.

1. German engineer Karl Humann discovered a 40-foot statue of Zeus sitting atop an 800-foot mountain in the middle of the city in 1878. The statue now resides in East Berlin.
2. The people of Pergamos also worshipped Athena, Dionysius, and Asclepius, the Greek god of medicine, represented today

as a serpent on a staff. Perhaps this symbol was why Christ called Pergamos a city "where Satan dwells" (Revelation 2:13).

Gamos

The Greek word *gamos* in the name Pergamos is the root for our English words related to marriage. *Monogamy* is "marriage to one person." *Polygamy* is "marriage to multiple people."

And as a play on words, Jesus' indictment of the church at Pergamos was that it had "married" the world. The people had adopted worldly practices and brought them into church, and thus, the church became more Roman than Christian. This was part of the beginning of the Roman Catholic Church.

Constantine's Epiphany

In AD 312, Emperor Constantine told of an epiphany he had one day when he went to war. He claimed he had a vision of a fiery cross in the sky and he heard, in Latin, the message, "In this sign, you will conquer." In response to that "vision," Constantine began to conquer in the name of Christ, using his newfound Christian faith as a weapon against enemy nations. He carved the heart out of Christianity, and people came under the rule of religion rather than into a relationship with Christ.

The World Enters the Church

Over time, more and more Roman culture infiltrated the church and subsequently introduced several erroneous practices, including:

1. The practice of praying for the dead
2. The doctrine of purgatory
3. The worship of saints and angels
4. The worship of Mary, exalting her for being the earthly mother of Jesus
5. The priestly attire of dress robes and clerical collars worn to separate the priests from the laity

Note that those who marry the world—who try to win the world by becoming like the world—have no distinction with which to attract the world.

Letter to Pergamos

1. The Greeting: Directed to the angel, or the pastor, of the church of Pergamos.

> **REVELATION 2:12a**–"To the angel of the church in Pergamos write…"

2. The Title for Jesus: Jesus' title alludes here to judgment.

> **REVELATION 2:12b**–"He who has the sharp two-edged sword…"

3. The Reminder:

> **REVELATION 2:13a**–"I know your works."

4. The Commendation: The saints at Pergamos were faithful to Christ despite their friend Antipas's death.

> **REVELATION 2:13**–"I know your works, and where you dwell, where Satan's throne is. And you hold fast to My name, and did not deny My faith even in the days in which Antipas was My faithful martyr, who was killed among you, where Satan dwells."

5. The Complaint: The church at Pergamos compromised with the world and allowed false doctrines into the church. Specifically, Christ called out the false doctrines of Balaam and the Nicolaitans.

REVELATION 2:14-15–"I have a few things against you, because you have there those who hold the doctrine of Balaam, who taught Balak to put a stumbling block before the children of Israel, to eat things sacrificed to idols, and to commit sexual immorality. Thus you also have those who hold the doctrine of the Nicolaitans, which thing I hate."

The Doctrine of Balaam

In Numbers 22, King Balak of Moab hired Balaam, who was an occult worshipper and a false prophet, and paid him to put a curse on Israel so that the Moabites might defeat the Israelites in battle. Despite this, Balaam was unable to curse the Jews because God had shut his mouth from pronouncing anything but blessings!

Imagine trying to curse a person who cuts you off on the highway, but only "Jesus loves you!" comes out of your mouth!

Realizing he would not be able to curse Israel, Balaam advised Balak to defeat the Israelites "from within." His recommended strategy was to remove God's blessings from the Israelites by getting the Moabite women to seduce the Israelite soldiers into sexual immorality.

Hence, the doctrine of Balaam represents moral compromise, idolatry, and greed.

The Doctrine of the Nicolaitans

Church tradition says this doctrine started with Nicolas, the deacon in Acts 6:5 who supposedly perverted the doctrine of grace by twisting it to mean that believers could live whatever way they wanted as long as they prayed and sought God. This theory states that those who followed Nicolas's view were known as Nicolaitans.

But more likely, as explained earlier about the letter to the church in Ephesus, this doctrine is rooted in the Greek meaning of the word "Nicolaitans," derived from the words *nikaó*, meaning "to conquer," and *laos*, meaning "the laity," which together means "to conquer the laity." This type of conquering happens when church leaders lord authority over the laity, and doing this is not biblical. Jesus Himself modeled servant leadership and taught against lording authority.

> Matthew 20:25-28—"Jesus called them to Himself and said, 'You know that the rulers of the Gentiles lord it over them, and those who are great exercise authority over them. Yet it shall not be so among you; but whoever desires to become great among you, let him be your servant. And whoever desires to be first among you, let him be your slave—just as the Son of Man did not come to be served, but to serve, and to give His life a ransom for many.'"

6. The Challenge: Listen.

> **REVELATION 2:17a**–"He who has an ear, let him hear what the Spirit says to the churches."

7. The Reward: God promised to give overcomers two things:

> **REVELATION 2:17b**–"To him who overcomes I will give some of the hidden manna to eat. And I will give him a white stone, and on the stone a new name written which no one knows except him who receives it."

First, Jesus is the "bread of life" (John 6:35), the "hidden manna," and the reward for overcoming.

Second, the symbolism of the white stone with our names written on it is that we are "accepted in the Beloved" (Ephesians 1:6).

White Stone

In Old Testament Israel, the high priest had the Urim and the Thummim to discern God's will. These were small stones kept within the priest's vestment. One stone was white, and one was black. When people came to the priest in search of an answer, they would ask a yes or no question, and the priest would pull out from his priestly vestment either the Urim, a white stone meaning "yes" or "acceptable," or the Thummim, a black stone meaning "no" or "unacceptable."

Of course, we, now, have the Holy Spirit and no longer use this method to discern God's will, but this was how He directed His people and communicated with them during Old Testament times. Thus, the white stone with our names written on it symbolizes God's affirmation and acceptance of us as His people.

New Name

As God renamed Jacob *Israel* after wrestling with him in Genesis 32:27-28, so we, too, will each receive a new name. Our new name, presently known only to Jesus, is a symbol of Christ's affection, a name that is unique to each of us in the way that God sees us.

Church at Thyatira

Chronologically, Thyatira represents the church from AD 606 to 1517. This age spans from the birth of the Roman Catholic Church to the birth of the Protestant church, when Martin Luther nailed the Ninety-Five Theses on the door of Castle Church at Wittenberg, Germany.

History of Thyatira

Regionally, Thyatira was situated approximately 30 miles between Sardis and Pergamos. This city was first established when Alexander the Great turned it into a Macedonian colony after the Persian Empire fell. Today, this area is the district of Akhisar and has a population of about 50,000.

Economically, Thyatira was known for its reddish-purple dye that is now referred to as Turkish red, a dye that comes from crushing a shellfish indigenous to the area. The sale of this commodity made the city famous.

In Acts 16:14, Lydia of Thyatira is mentioned as being a dealer of purple cloth.

Besides this, Thyatira was a heavily industrialized city and therefore had more commercial guilds than any other Roman province. Thyatira had guilds for dyers, wool workers, linen workers, leather workers, tanners, potters, bakers, and bronzesmiths.

The city prospered. But spiritually, Thyatira was riddled with idolatry.

Roman Catholic Church Emerges

The Roman Catholic Church began to emerge in AD 606, though the Catholics deny this and say that the apostle Peter was their first pope. However, Catholicism as we know it has its roots in the following events:

1. Constantine legalized Christianity, and Theodosius made Christianity a state religion and elevated bishops to oversee the different churches in the Roman Empire.
2. Bishop Sabinian died, and Boniface III rose in his place.
3. Emperor Phocas wrote to Boniface III, making him, by imperial edict, the universal bishop over all the churches and bishops of the Roman Empire.

While the Western Roman Empire believed Rome should be the capital city, the Eastern Roman Empire disagreed, and a centuries-long power struggle followed till the empire split in AD 395. This divided empire, held together only by religion, split again in AD 1054, when the Eastern Orthodox Church in the east separated itself from the Roman Catholic Church in the west.

Extrabiblical Traditions

The time following AD 606 also introduced many extrabiblical doctrines practiced by the Catholic Church:

1. The ritual kissing of the pope's feet.
2. The use of holy water.
3. The practice of praying with rosary beads, invented by Peter the Hermit in AD 1090.
4. The doctrine of transubstantiation, which is the belief that

the communion elements miraculously become the actual flesh and blood of Christ, in AD 1215. Catholic doctrine interprets John 6:48-58 as a literal command to eat Jesus' flesh and to drink His blood, despite how Jesus clarified this, saying in John 6:63: "It is the Spirit who gives life; the flesh profits nothing. The words that I speak to you are spirit, and they are life." Therefore, we understand John 6:48-58 to speak of communion in a spiritual sense rather than a literal sense; that is, the spiritual consumption of all that Jesus is rather than relegating Him to the fringe of our lives.

5. The belief that the Bible could only be interpreted by priests, and therefore was forbidden to laymen, in AD 1229. In fact, this distance between the priests and laymen was furthered because Catholic Mass was conducted in Latin until the mid-1960s. But these things are not biblical. God's Word tells us:

   1 Corinthians 2:13—The Spirit in us interprets God's Word.

   1 Timothy 2:5—There is only one mediator between God and man, the Man Christ Jesus.

   Acts 17:11—Laymen can and should double-check everything they hear with Scripture, as the Bereans did. For this, they earned Paul's commendation.

God encourages us to grow by studying His Word, and we are blessed with Bibles we can read for ourselves, study guide resources, and Greek and Hebrew lexicons.

Letter to Thyatira

1. The Greeting: Directed to the angel, or pastor, of the church at Thyatira.

> **REVELATION 2:18a**–"To the angel of the church in Thyatira write…"

2. The Title for Jesus: Jesus introduced Himself as the righteous Judge.

> **REVELATION 2:18b**–"The Son of God, who has eyes like a flame of fire…"

The eyes of fire show that He was angry.

> **REVELATION 2:18b**–"His feet like fine brass…"

In Scripture, brass or bronze symbolizes judgment.

3. The Reminder:

> **REVELATION 2:19a**–"I know your works."

4. The Commendation: Jesus commended the believers at Thyatira for five things, including their love, which is a commendation no previous church received.

> **REVELATION 2:19**–"I know your works, love, service, faith, and your patience; and as for your works, the last are more than the first."

The word for "service" here is the Greek term *diakonos*, from which we get our English word *deacon*. Jesus commended the believers of Thyatira for their service. They ministered to, served, and loved people, and did all this with faith and patience.

However, Jesus held a great complaint against them.

5. The Complaint: They tolerated sin; specifically, they allowed into the church the corruption of Jezebel.

REVELATION 2:20—"Nevertheless I have a few things against you, because you allow that woman Jezebel, who calls herself a prophetess, to teach and seduce My servants to commit sexual immorality and eat things sacrificed to idols."

The Symbolism of Jezebel

The term "Jezebel" could refer to how Thyatira had a temple of fortune-tellers presided over by a powerful female oracle, and this oracle could be the Jezebel in Jesus' letter.

However, "Jezebel" also has Old Testament connotations that have led some to believe the sin of Jezebel at Thyatira relates to the church being seduced by the world system with its idolatrous practices.

First Kings 16 tells us of Queen Jezebel, wife of Ahab, a pagan, idolatrous woman. We also know she was the daughter of King Ethbaal of the Sidonians ("Ethbaal" means "with Baal") and was steeped in idolatry from childhood. The first-century Roman historian Josephus said that her father, Ethbaal, was a priest of the occult. Jezebel took after him, introducing pagan practices to God's people and seducing them into idol worship (2 Kings 9:22). Because of this, she became a symbol of witchcraft and idolatry.

Not to disparage Catholics, but whether Jezebel refers to a literal or symbolic woman, the Roman Catholic Church is as steeped in idolatry as Jezebel was through their icons, statues, idolization of Mary, and ritual praying to the saints.

Of course, within the Catholic Church there are true believers, just as there are in other denominations, but they belong to a misguided religious circle.

The Judgment of Jezebel

The Roman Catholic Church's rightful reverence for Jesus as Savior combined with sinful, idolatrous practices creates a corrupt religious system.

> **REVELATION 2:21-22**–"I gave her [Jezebel] time to repent of her sexual immorality, and she did not repent. Indeed I will cast her into a sickbed, and those who commit adultery with her into great tribulation, unless they repent of their deeds."

The verses above suggest that those within the church who are found in spiritual fornication—that is, those who believe in adding works to grace and in worshipping idols over God—do not have a real, personal relationship with Christ and will thus suffer through the tribulation to come.

6. The Challenge: Listen.

> **REVELATION 2:29**–"He who has an ear, let him hear what the Spirit says to the churches."

7. The Reward: Jesus promised to reward the faithful remnant.

> **REVELATION 2:24-25**–"Now to you I say, and to the rest in Thyatira, as many as do not have this doctrine, who have not known the depths of Satan, as they say, I will put on you no other burden. But hold fast what you have till I come."

God always has a remnant, and He bids those who belong to Him to hold fast to Him until He returns.

And the reward is twofold. First, He promises to give the faithful authority over the nations:

> **REVELATION 2:26-27**–"He who overcomes, and keeps My works until the end, to him I will give power over the nations—'He shall rule them with a rod of iron; they shall be dashed to pieces like the potter's vessels'—as I also have received from My Father."

Revelation 20:4—"I saw thrones, and they sat on them, and judgment was committed to them. Then I saw the souls of those who had been beheaded for their witness to Jesus and for the word of God, who had not worshiped the beast or his image, and had not received his mark on their foreheads or on their hands. And they lived and reigned with Christ for a thousand years."

Second, He promised the faithful the greatest reward: Himself.

REVELATION 2:28–"I will give him the morning star."

Revelation 22:16—"I, Jesus, have sent My angel to testify to you these things in the churches. I am the Root and the Offspring of David, the Bright and Morning Star."

Malachi 4:2—"To you who fear My name the Sun of Righteousness shall arise with healing in His wings; and you shall go out and grow fat like stall-fed calves."

Reflections on Revelation 2

Getting Started

What seven elements were present in Jesus' letters to the seven churches? How can we benefit from applying these elements to our own lives and churches today?

Study Questions

1. What reminder did Jesus give to each of the seven churches (Revelation 2:2, 9, 13, 19; 3:1, 8, 15)? How might this reminder influence your Christian walk?
2. Jesus commended the church of Ephesus for hating the doctrine of the Nicolaitans. What does this doctrine teach? Today, some teach that we need priests or others to represent us before God, but who does 1 Timothy 2:5 say is the only mediator between us and God?
3. What is the symbolic significance of Smyrna's myrrh trade?
4. What makes the church at Smyrna—and all believers—rich regardless of circumstances (Revelation 2:9)? What are some ways we can exhibit this trait today?
5. What is the heresy of the Judaizers? What are some ways you have seen this heresy sneak into Christianity?
6. The church at Smyrna was too busy doing God's work to get into trouble, so Smyrna is one of two churches to not be rebuked by Jesus. What can we learn from the church at Smyrna?
7. What root problem did Constantine introduce when he legalized Christianity, which led to ushering in the state church? What practices ended up entering the church at this time?

8. Jesus' complaint against the church at Pergamos was that the believers had married the world. What are some examples you have seen of Christianity marrying today's culture? What are some ways to avoid this trap?
9. By what title did Jesus introduce Himself to the church at Thyatira (Revelation 2:18)? How should this influence the way we live?
10. In Jesus' letter to the church at Thyatira, what does Jezebel represent? What does His complaint against Thyatira in relation to Jezebel tell us about His expectations of us?

Important Takeaways for Us Today

1. The believers in the church at Smyrna were rich because of their faithfulness. Below are some other riches we enjoy as believers. For each item below, share how you have experienced that aspect of God's riches in your life:
   a. **Romans 2:4**—The riches of His kindness
   b. **Romans 9:23**—The riches of His glory
   c. **Romans 11:33**—The riches of His wisdom and knowledge
   d. **Ephesians 1:7**—The riches of His grace
   e. **Ephesians 1:18**—The riches of our glorious inheritance
   f. **Ephesians 3:8**—The unsearchable riches of Christ

2. In Revelation 2:26-28, Jesus made two promises to the faithful: He promised authority over the nations, and He promised Himself. Why do you think Jesus places so much importance on our faithfulness? What are some ways we can show our faithfulness to Him?

3

Letters to Our Age

REVELATION 3

The church in Sardis is known as the "dead church" because the church members' spiritual lives failed to stand apart from the darkness around them. In this chapter, we will study the symbolism in Christ's letter to Sardis and how the great awakenings and the woke revolution of our times fit into the timeline detailed in Revelation.

Church at Sardis

Chronologically, Sardis represents the church from 1517–1750, covering the time from the Protestant Reformation to the Great Awakening that birthed the evangelical church.

History of Sardis

Sardis was 50 miles east of Smyrna and 30 miles southeast of Thyatira, placing it along a major trade route through Asia Minor, where it thrived as the center of carpet, wool, and clothing industries during the first century. Sardis was a wealthy city and some of the first coins were minted there.

And like the other cities in the Roman Empire, Sardis was polytheistic, with its main deities being Artemis, goddess of the hunt; Cybele, goddess of the earth; and Dionysus, the god of wine.

Sardis was also known for having a huge necropolis—that is, a large graveyard. This stemmed from the people's worship of Cybele, whom they believed could restore the dead to life. The word *necropolis* stems from two Greek words: *necros*, meaning "death," and *polis*, meaning "city." Hence, Sardis was nicknamed "the cemetery on a thousand hills." Amid this pagan culture, the church was a testimony, and the remains of an early Christian church were found beside the temple to Artemis.

In AD 17, an earthquake devastated Sardis and the city was never rebuilt to its former glory. Today, the town is called Sart and has a population of about 5,300.

Pivotal Moments in Church History

Protestantism began with Martin Luther, who disagreed with the Roman Catholic Church, especially in the areas of works and indulgences, or the act of paying priests to absolve you of your sins. These indulgences were considered "payment for pardon" and disturbed Luther enough that he nailed his *Ninety-Five Theses* on the door of Castle Church in Wittenberg, Germany, detailing his disagreements and launching the Protestant Reformation. Luther's *Theses* were then translated from Latin to German and spread rapidly around Europe.

A copy was sent to Rome, and the clergy tried to convince Luther to retract his stance. He did not. Thus in 1521, Pope Leo X excommunicated Luther from the Catholic Church. That same year, Luther stood before the Holy Roman Emperor Charles V of Germany and refused to recant his writings, so the emperor issued the Edict of Worms, a decree that condemned Luther as a heretic and an outlaw. This decree gave anyone the right to kill Martin Luther without consequence.

However, Prince Frederick III protected Luther, and Luther spent about 12 years completing a German translation of the Bible.

Then, from 1517 to the mid-1700s, the Protestant church formed. The evangelical church eventually emerged from this movement, beginning with the First Great Awakening.

Letter to Sardis

1. The Greeting: Directed to the angel, or pastor, of the church at Sardis.

REVELATION 3:1a–"To the angel of the church in Sardis write..."

2. The Title for Jesus:

REVELATION 3:1b–"He who has the seven Spirits of God and the seven stars..."

Seven Spirits

The number seven in the Bible is a symbol of perfection or completion, and therefore some theorize that the "seven Spirits of God" simply refers to the perfect work of the Holy Spirit.

Others believe that this phrase refers to the sevenfold Spirit, or the complete fullness of the Spirit mentioned in Isaiah:

> **Isaiah 11:2**—"The Spirit of the LORD shall rest upon Him, the Spirit of wisdom and understanding, the Spirit of counsel and might, the Spirit of knowledge and of the fear of the LORD."

Notice this passage refers to seven attributes of the singular Holy Spirit:

- the Spirit of the Lord
- the Spirit of wisdom
- the Spirit of understanding
- the Spirit of counsel
- the Spirit of might
- the Spirit of knowledge
- the Spirit of the fear of the Lord

3. The Reminder:

> **REVELATION 3:1c**—"I know your works."

4. The Commendation: Jesus commended the faithful few.

> **REVELATION 3:4a**—"You have a few names even in Sardis who have not defiled their garments."

God does not need many to accomplish His purposes.

5. The Complaint: They were alive on the outside, but dead on the inside. Activity does not equal vitality. Their works were not done out of the overflow of their walk with God.

> **REVELATION 3:1c**—"You have a name that you are alive, but you are dead."

6. The Challenge: Listen.

> **REVELATION 3:6**—"He who has an ear, let him hear what the Spirit says to the churches."

7. The Reward: Jesus promised the overcomers three things.

First, they will walk with Him in white. White represents purity, so the white garments represent how God will clothe us in His own righteousness.

> **REVELATION 3:4b-5a**—"They shall walk with Me in white, for they are worthy. He who overcomes shall be clothed in white garments."

Second, God will not blot out their names from the Book of Life.

> **REVELATION 3:5b**—"I will not blot out his name from the Book of Life; but I will confess his name before My Father and before His angels."

Third, Jesus will confess their names before His Father and the angels.

The Book of Life

This book is mentioned seven times in the New King James Version, and this reference is the first. The Bible tells us this book records the names of all individuals who will go to heaven when they die or are raptured.

Notice, John did not say the righteous will be added to the Book of Life. The implication is that everyone's name starts out in the Book of Life and gets blotted out if he or she rejects Christ.

> **Psalm 69:28**—"Let them be blotted out of the book of the living, and not be written with the righteous."

This inference answers the question often asked: What happens to those who die young or who have mental disabilities that prevent them from understanding the gospel and accepting Christ? They go to be with the Lord.

Another passage that supports this view is in 2 Samuel. When David's infant son was deathly ill, David prayed and fasted. But when the baby died, note how David responded.

> **2 Samuel 12:23**—"Now he is dead; why should I fast? Can I bring him back again? I shall go to him, but he shall not return to me."

David believed he and the baby were going to the same afterlife, and that he would see his son again!

Church at Philadelphia

Chronologically, Philadelphia represents the faithful church from the time of the First Great Awakening of 1750 to the present day.

This church exists simultaneously with the church at Laodicea. At the turn of the twentieth century, liberal theology crept into the Protestant church, creating two diverging paths: evangelical Christianity and liberal theology. Laodicea symbolizes the apostate church, and Philadelphia symbolizes the evangelical church, which will one day be raptured.

The Evangelical Shift

After the emergence of Protestantism, there was another great shift in church history—the First Great Awakening. This movement stimulated the growth of several educational institutions, including Princeton, Brown, Rutgers, and Dartmouth.

Because this movement diverged from the state churches, it led the push for greater religious freedom. This push eventually led the American colonies to decide to rise against the religious intolerance of England, culminating in the American Revolution.

The Great Awakenings

Church history includes four great awakenings:

1. 1730–1740—The leaders of the First Great Awakening included George Whitefield, Jonathan Edwards, and John and Charles Wesley. John Wesley logged over 250,000 miles on horseback, preaching the gospel throughout Scotland and England.
2. 1790–1840—During the Second Great Awakening, there were conversions of about 10,000 people a week in New York City; church bells were calling people to prayer at 8:00 a.m., 12:00 noon, and 6:00 p.m. in New England; and Baptists were cutting holes in the ice-covered Hudson and Mohawk Rivers to baptize people. By 1857, more than one million

people were converted. The effects of this worldwide revival were felt for 40 years.

3. 1855–1930—The Third Great Awakening included the Welsh revival (1904–1905). Dr. John Shiver, in *The Glory of His Presence*, wrote that this powerful move of God was evident in the cessation of prostitution, bars and gambling houses closing from lack of business, and courthouses closing because there were no criminal cases to try. All social indicators improved—a glimpse into what life in the millennium would be like!
4. 1960–1980—The Fourth Great Awakening of the 1970s and 1980s included Billy Graham revivals, the Charismatic Renewal, and the Jesus movement led by Calvary Chapel and Pastor Chuck Smith.

Historically, there has been a great awakening every 30 to 40 years. We are due for another!

History of Philadelphia

Philadelphia, Greek for "the city of brotherly love," was built by and named after King Attalus II Philadelphus of Pergamos, who died in 138 BC. Philadelphia is now Alaşehir, Turkey, which is derived from the Arabic words *ălă′*, meaning "God," and *shĕhēr′*, meaning "city," together meaning "the city of God." It is now an Islamic city.

But back in John's time, Philadelphia was given over to the worship of Dionysus, the god of wine, also called Bacchus by the Romans. Situated on the volcanic slopes of Mount Tmolus, the city had fertile soil for growing grapes and producing wine.

Bacchus was also the god of revelry, and his worshippers held an annual feast that included drunken orgies in his name. Yet against this pagan background, a Christian church thrived.

Little is known about Philadelphia, for the city was rocked and devastated by several earthquakes and was almost destroyed by the same earthquake that ruined Sardis in AD 17.

Letter to Philadelphia

1. The Greeting: Directed to the angel, or pastor, of the church at Philadelphia.

> **REVELATION 3:7a**–"To the angel of the church in Philadelphia write…"

2. The Title for Jesus: God is holy and true, and the rightful heir to the throne of David.

> **REVELATION 3:7b**–"He who is holy, He who is true, 'He who has the key of David, He who opens and no one shuts, and shuts and no one opens…'"

First, Jesus is holy and true. There are two Greek words for "true." One means "true and not false," and the other means "true and not fake." The latter is used here, *alēthinos*, and it helps us to understand that Jesus is real, genuine, and true in every aspect.

Second, He is the "key of David" who opens doors that no man can shut and closes doors that no man can open. This phrase references a passage in Isaiah.

> **Isaiah 22:22**—"The key of the house of David I will lay on his shoulder; so he shall open, and no one shall shut; and he shall shut, and no one shall open."

Jesus is asserting His authority as David's rightful heir.

3. The Reminder:

> **REVELATION 3:8a**–"I know your works."

4. The Commendation: They had little strength yet were faithful to God's Word.

REVELATION 3:8b-9–"See, I have set before you an open door, and no one can shut it; for you have a little strength, have kept My word, and have not denied My name. Indeed I will make those of the synagogue of Satan, who say they are Jews and are not, but lie—indeed I will make them come and worship before your feet, and to know that I have loved you."

This was not an arrogant church. The people knew their limits, and clung to God and refused to deny Him. Jesus also commended them for keeping God's Word despite persecution.

5. The Complaint: Philadelphia received no complaint, making it one of only two churches for which Jesus had no indictment. This is the ideal church, the evangelical church.
6. The Challenge: Listen.

REVELATION 3:13–"He who has an ear, let him hear what the Spirit says to the churches."

7. The Reward: The saints at Philadelphia will be kept from the hour of trial that is coming upon the world.

REVELATION 3:10-11–"Because you have kept My command to persevere, I also will keep you from the hour of trial which shall come upon the whole world, to test those who dwell on the earth. Behold, I am coming quickly! Hold fast what you have, that no one may take your crown."

This time of trial is mentioned in various other Bible passages:

- Jeremiah 30:7 refers to this period as "the time of Jacob's trouble."
- Daniel 9:27 refers to it as Daniel's seventieth week.
- Matthew 24:21 refers to it as "great tribulation, such as has

> not been since the beginning of the world until this time, no, nor ever shall be."

Jesus' promised reward is proof that His true followers will escape the hour of trial that will come upon the whole world, the great tribulation. And this promise is not the only proof:

> **1 Thessalonians 4**—Paul mentioned the rapture, saying that those who are alive and remain will be caught in the air with Him at the sound of a trumpet.
>
> **1 Thessalonians 5**—Paul prophesied about the intensity of the tribulation, but then said in verse 9, "God did not appoint us to wrath."

God will graciously rescue us from the great tribulation. May we continue to witness to an unbelieving world so that people may escape the hour of trouble with us.

Church at Laodicea

Symbolically, Laodicea represents the apostate church from 1750 to the present day, covering the time from the Great Awakening till now.

The church at Laodicea symbolizes the liberal church that discounts the claims of Christ and denies the foundations of the faith, for which the people will face the tribulation. Not all who claim to know Christ truly know Him.

History of Laodicea

Antiochus II founded Laodicea around 246 BC and named the city after his wife Laodice. By the first century, the population of Laodicea was 17,000 strong. Today, it bears the Arabic name *Eskihisar*, meaning "old castle."

Laodicea was a wealthy city 40 miles southeast of Philadelphia, situated along a major Asian trade route along the Lycus Valley. The area was known for a breed of sheep that produced glossy, black wool useful for making fine, expensive coats. It was also known for its medical school and the discovery of boric acid, which was used in eye salves.

But despite Laodicea's wealth, fresh drinking water was scarce and had to be piped in through aqueducts, specifically from the Hierapolis hot springs to the north. But by the time the water reached Laodicea, it was lukewarm.

The church at Laodicea is mentioned four times in Colossians, and we know Paul wrote to the people there (Colossians 4:16), but we have no record of it.

Letter to Laodicea

1. The Greeting: Directed to the angel, or pastor, of the church at Laodicea.

> **REVELATION 3:14a**–"To the angel of the church of the Laodiceans write..."

2. The Title for Jesus:

> **REVELATION 3:14b**–"The Amen, the Faithful and True Witness, the Beginning of the creation of God..."

First, Jesus called Himself the Amen, meaning His words are reliable and true. "Amen" can be translated as "verily," "I tell you the truth," or "so be it."

Second, He called Himself "the Faithful and True Witness," speaking of His accurate and reliable Word.

And third, He called Himself "the Beginning of the creation of God." The NIV Bible says, "the ruler of God's creation." This title emphasizes Jesus' preeminence and pre-existence.

> **Colossians 1:16**—"By Him all things were created that are in heaven and that are on earth, visible and invisible, whether thrones or dominions or principalities or powers. All things were created through Him and for Him."

3. The Reminder:

> **REVELATION 3:15a**–"I know your works."

4. The Commendation: This is the only church to receive no commendation from Jesus.
5. The Complaint: Jesus complained that the people were lukewarm and too proud to come to God.

A Lukewarm Church

Jesus referred to them spiritually as "lukewarm," a play on words referring to the city's lukewarm drinking water after it travelled the distance from the hot springs of Hierapolis to Laodicea.

> **REVELATION 3:15b-16**–"You are neither cold nor hot. I could wish you were cold or hot. So then, because you are lukewarm, and neither cold nor hot, I will vomit you out of My mouth."

If you are hot and on fire for God, great. And if you are cold, at least God has something to work with. But if you are lukewarm, God finds it distasteful and of no advantage to the kingdom.

Skip Heitzig, the pastor of Calvary Church in Albuquerque, New Mexico, describes the characteristics that define a lukewarm Christian:

> To be spiritually lukewarm is to be complacent, halfhearted, and unable to recognize the depth of one's spiritual need. The lukewarm person straddles the fence and is halfhearted about spiritual things. Conviction never affects his or her conscious level; the conscience remains untouched. Lukewarm people don't take either Jesus or the Bible seriously. They wink at sin and have no concern for a lost world; hence they have no viable witness.[1]

Prideful Independence

In essence, Jesus rebuked the lukewarm Laodiceans because they were pridefully self-sufficient.

In fact, when the government offered to help fund Laodicea's rebuilding project after an earthquake in AD 60 demolished the city, the Laodiceans declined. They thought their money from the wool trade would suffice.

The people had an admirable entrepreneurial spirit, but this crept into the church so much so that they overestimated themselves and underestimated God.

> **REVELATION 3:17**–"You say, 'I am rich, have become wealthy, and have need of nothing'—and do not know that you are wretched, miserable, poor, blind, and naked."

Jesus then told them they needed to be clothed in Him to cover their spiritual nakedness, and they needed His eye salve to fix their spiritual blindness.

> **REVELATION 3:18**–"I counsel you to buy from Me gold refined in the fire, that you may be rich; and white garments, that you may be clothed, that the shame of your nakedness may not be revealed; and anoint your eyes with eye salve, that you may see."

In this verse are multiple plays on words. The Laodiceans were known for their wealth, but Christ wanted them to become rich in Him. They were famous for their glossy, black wool coats, but Christ wanted them to be clothed in His righteousness. They were known for their eye salves, but Christ wanted them to have His spiritual sight.

6. The Challenge: Listen

> **REVELATION 3:22**–"He who has an ear, let him hear what the Spirit says to the churches."

7. The Reward: Fellowship with Christ and a place beside Him on His throne.

I Stand at the Door

Despite the lukewarm manner of the Laodiceans, Jesus called them to repent. Even the most wayward person can come to Christ.

> **REVELATION 3:20**—"Behold, I stand at the door and knock. If anyone hears My voice and opens the door, I will come in to him and dine with him, and he with Me."

In Warner Sallman's 1942 painting *Christ at Heart's Door*, Sallman intentionally left out a doorknob on the outside of the door, indicating how we, from the inside, have the choice about whether to open the "door of our heart" to Christ. Jesus does not force His way in. He knocks and waits for us to accept or reject His plea to fellowship with Him.

I Will Grant to Sit with Me

Jesus longs to share His inheritance rights and eternity with us.

> **REVELATION 3:21**—"To him who overcomes I will grant to sit with Me on My throne, as I also overcame and sat down with My Father on His throne."

> **Romans 8:17**—"If children, then heirs—heirs of God and joint heirs with Christ, if indeed we suffer with Him, that we may also be glorified together."

Apostasy of Laodicea

During the twentieth century, many theologians determined God was narrow-minded, as if they were more enlightened than God. As

Jesus predicted, they allowed culture to shape the church instead of encouraging the church to shape the culture:

> **Matthew 24:10**—"Many will be offended, will betray one another, and will hate one another."
>
> **1 Timothy 4:1**—"Now the Spirit expressly says that in latter times some will depart from the faith, giving heed to deceiving spirits and doctrines of demons."
>
> **2 Timothy 4:3**—"The time will come when they will not endure sound doctrine, but according to their own desires, because they have itching ears, they will heap up for themselves teachers."

This liberal, secular infiltration of the church came in waves:

Humanism

The Enlightenment era infiltrated colleges from 1600 to 1830, and these schools abandoned their Christian foundations for philosophies by humanists like Descartes, Voltaire, Diderot, Hobbes, Locke, George Berkeley, Kant, Paine, David Hume, and John Stuart Mill. These philosophers considered religion, and Christianity especially, to be barbaric and irrelevant.

Liberal Theology

German liberal theologians like Albrecht Ritschl, who believed that the Bible was not true in its totality, began to create doubt about the inerrancy of God's Word.

Darwinism

In 1859, Darwin published *On the Origin of Species*. After him came influential Darwinian figures like Aldous Huxley, Engels, Marx, Freud, George Herbert Mead, Max Weber, Oliver Wendell Holmes, Roscoe Pound, John Dewey, B.F. Skinner, and Charles W. Eliot.

Tolerance

In 1922, Harry Emerson Fosdick declared, in a sermon to the Northern Baptist Convention, that Christianity did not need the intolerance of fundamentalists, but rather, the tolerance of diverse belief practiced by enlightened modernists, thus casting doubt on absolute truth.

Secularism

By the 1930s, the Ivy League schools had fallen to secularism, even becoming hostile to religions of any kind.

Naturalism

In 2000, secular historians Jon H. Roberts and James Turner published *The Sacred and The Secular University*, in which they discussed universities turning from a Christian to a naturalistic philosophy.

The results are clear: Embracing liberal and secular thought and tolerating and celebrating sin under the banner of love have led to an erosion of Christianity from the culture.

Reflections on Revelation 3

Getting Started

In Revelation 3, Jesus gave a message to three churches living in pagan lands. While these three churches resided in similar cultural contexts, they were different in how they responded to their environments. The church at Philadelphia lived in a manner that earned no complaint from Christ, the church at Laodicea lived in a manner that earned no commendation from Christ, and the church at Sardis lived with a mix of both. How can we rise above our environments to live for Christ?

Study Questions

1. Contrast Jesus' commendation for Philadelphia (Revelation 3:8) and complaint against Laodicea (Revelation 3:17). What would Christ say about you or your church in relation to today's culture? How should we allow God to impact our spiritual walk?
2. The church at Sardis was full of activity, but dead inside. How do you ensure that your work is not merely activity?
3. In Revelation 3:5, Jesus promised to overcomers that He would not blot out their names from the Book of Life, not that He would add them in. What does this promise imply?
4. Jesus introduced Himself to Philadelphia as "He who is true" (Revelation 3:7). What does the Greek word for "true" tell us about the character and nature of God?
5. What does Philadelphia teach us to do when we have only "a little strength" (Revelation 3:8)?
6. What reward did Jesus promise the church at Philadelphia in Revelation 3:10-11? How does this promise apply to us?
7. What did Jesus assert about Himself by saying He is "the

Amen" (Revelation 3:14)? How does this attribute of God give you peace?

8. The church at Laodicea was rich and known for their wool coats and eye salve, but Jesus called them poor, blind, and naked (Revelation 3:17-18). What points did Jesus make with His use of irony?
9. In Revelation 3:20, Jesus told the church at Laodicea that He stands at the door and knocks. What is the significance of Jesus knocking rather than barging in?
10. In Revelation 3:21, Jesus made a grand promise to overcomers. How does the Bible define an "overcomer" (see Romans 8:17)?

Important Takeaways for Us Today

1. Review Skip Heitzig's list of seven characteristics that define a lukewarm Christian. Do any of these seven apply to you? What is the simple first step toward reigniting your love for God (Revelation 3:20)?
2. How do the churches at Philadelphia and Laodicea symbolize the diverging strands of modern Christianity? How can we beware of the spirit of apostasy in ourselves and our churches?

4

The Throne in Heaven

REVELATION 4

Have you ever met a king? If you are a believer in Jesus Christ, one day you will. The Bible says that for believers, to be absent from the body is to be present with the Lord (2 Corinthians 5:8). This is our hope: To be with Him who is worshipped by angels and saints. And in Revelation chapter 4, we get a glimpse of Jesus, whose appearance is like "jasper and a sardius stone" (verse 3). Until then, we wait with great expectation for the *harpazō*, the rapture of the church.

Revelation in Three Parts

Revelation is divided into three parts: past, present, and future.

> **Revelation 1:19**—"Write the things which you have seen, and the things which are, and the things which will take place after this."

In chapter 1, John first wrote about the things he saw, including the vision of Jesus.

In chapters 2 and 3, John moved on to the things that are—present tense—and this encompasses the church age, which began with Jesus' ascension and continues unto this day.

In chapters 4 through 22, John wrote about things that will shortly take place after this. The two words "after this" are *meta tauta* in the Greek text; this refers to future events. Although a few events after chapter 4 are set in the past, from here on out, Revelation covers mostly the things that are to come.

> **REVELATION 4:1**–"*After these things* I looked, and behold, a door standing open in heaven. And the first voice which I heard was like a trumpet speaking with me, saying, 'Come up here, and I will show you things which must take place *after this*.'"

John began with the phrase "after these things" and ended with the phrase "things which must take place after this," bookending verse 1 with meta tauta to cue us into Revelation's shift toward future events.

Future Events

John Transported

John was given an invitation, and he was transported to see future events.

> **REVELATION 4:2**–"Immediately I was in the Spirit; and behold, a throne set in heaven, and One sat on the throne."

What John Saw

Revelation 6–18 describes cataclysmic global events that will occur during the great tribulation, including wars, famine, economic collapse, natural disasters, earthquakes, meteor showers, hail, and fire. During these short seven years, billions will die.

God will allow these catastrophes for the sake of those who are too stubborn to yield to Christ. God, in His great compassion, will resort to the great tribulation in His final call to awaken a God-rejecting world. This will be man's last chance.

And though believers differ in their eschatological views—that is, in their beliefs about end-times events—I believe the church will be gone during the judgment of the world. God will remove us before the tribulation.

The Rapture

There are three primary views:

1. Post-tribulation—The belief that the church will be raptured after the tribulation.

> **John 16:33**—"These things I have spoken to you, that in Me you may have peace. In the world you will have tribulation; but be of good cheer, I have overcome the world."

"Tribulation" here does not refer to the great tribulation, but to the trials we face daily as believers.

2. Mid-tribulation—The belief that the church will be raptured in the middle of the tribulation.

> **Matthew 24:22**—"Unless those days were shortened, no flesh would be saved; but for the elect's sake those days will be shortened."

Those who hold to this view believe that because Christ said "shortened" rather than "avoided," Christians will face part of the tribulation, though not the worst of it.

3. Pre-tribulation—The belief that the church will be raptured before the tribulation.

> **Revelation 4:1-2**—John's call by the trumpet of God to join Jesus in heaven is a picture of the church getting raptured at the sound of the trumpet before the tribulation begins.

This is the view that I hold.

The Meaning of the Rapture

The rapture is the sudden return of Christ in the clouds to "take up" Christians from the earth to be with Him in heaven. This could happen at any time!

Some argue against the rapture because the word *rapture* is not found in the Bible. But neither is the word *Trinity* in Scripture, and yet both doctrines are clearly presented in God's Word.

The Importance of the Rapture

Knowing that Jesus is coming to take believers home is the blessed hope of the church.

The Etymology of the Rapture

It is true that the word *rapture* is not in the Bible, but the phrase "caught up" is.

> **1 Thessalonians 4:17**—"We who are alive and remain shall be caught up together with them in the clouds to meet the Lord in the air. And thus we shall always be with the Lord."

"Caught up" is *harpazō* in the Greek text, meaning "seized" or "snatched." And when the Bible was translated to Latin, the Greek word *harpazō* became the Latin word *raptus*, which means "to be seized, or caught up." We get our English word *rapture* from the Latin word *raptus*.

Those Who Remain

This describes the Christians living on Earth during the time Christ comes to rapture His church.

> **1 Thessalonians 4:15**—"This we say to you by the word of the Lord, that we who are alive and remain until the coming of the Lord will by no means precede those who are asleep."

At that time, all believers on Earth will be raptured, or caught up, to be with Jesus. The event will be announced with a great shout, the voice of an archangel, the sound of God's trumpet.

> **1 Thessalonians 4:16**—"The Lord Himself will descend from heaven with a shout, with the voice of an archangel, and with the trumpet of God. And the dead in Christ will rise first."

And those alive during the rapture will be given glorified bodies on the way up to heaven.

> **1 Corinthians 15:51-52**—"Behold, I tell you a mystery: We shall not all sleep, but we shall all be changed—in a moment, in the twinkling of an eye, at the last trumpet. For the trumpet will sound, and the dead will be raised incorruptible, and we shall be changed."

Those Who Sleep

This is an early church euphemism for death. "They will rise first" means that those saints who have gone on to heaven before us will be given their glorified bodies (to be reunited with their spirits in heaven) *immediately before* the living are raptured.

The Bible says once we die, we go immediately to the Lord's presence.

> **2 Corinthians 5:8**—"We are confident, yes, well pleased rather to be absent from the body and to be present with the Lord."

The God who made the heavens and the earth will construct glorified bodies for those who have died in Christ, whether they have been cremated, scattered at sea, or have naturally decomposed. God will gather the dust of each believer and miraculously form glorified bodies for those souls who are already with Him.

Comfort with These Words

The doctrine of the rapture is intended to comfort us.

> **1 Thessalonians 4:18**—"Therefore comfort one another with these words."

Jesus Speaks of the Rapture

In Matthew 24:37 and Luke 17:28-36, the rapture is compared to the days of Noah and Lot, noting that one will be taken (the saved) and the other left (unsaved). In each event, God intervenes to save His people from perishing with the unrighteous.

The Absence of the Word Church

The word *church* is mentioned 19 times in Revelation chapters 1–3 but disappears from the book until Revelation 22:16, after the tribulation is complete. This indicates the church will be absent from Earth during Revelation 6–18.

The Open Door in Heaven

At the start of chapter 4, John saw "a door standing open in heaven" (Revelation 4:1a). The only other time heaven is standing open is when Jesus ascends after His resurrection. And once again, heaven will be opened as Jesus prepares to descend to the earth.

> **Revelation 19:11**—"Now I saw heaven opened, and behold, a white horse. And He who sat on him was called Faithful and True, and in righteousness He judges and makes war."

This implies that an open door to heaven in Revelation 4 refers to how the "portal" to heaven is open to allow the saints to go up.

The Trump of God

John described God's voice as sounding like a trumpet, which is consistent with Scripture's account of what happens prior to the church's rapture.

> **Revelation 4:1b**—"The first voice which I heard was like a trumpet."
>
> **1 Thessalonians 4:16**—Refers to "the trumpet of God" sounding prior to the rapture.
>
> **1 Corinthians 15:51-52**—Says that believers will go up "at the last trumpet."

Come Up Here

God invited John to come up to heaven with Him in what appears to be either a vision or a spiritual transportation of some kind, similar to how Paul was caught up to the "third heaven" in 2 Corinthians 12:2.

> **Revelation 4:1c**—"Come up here, and I will show you things which must take place after this."

The only other time God calls for anyone to come up is in Revelation 11, when He invites the two witnesses to ascend to heaven.

> **Revelation 11:12**—"They heard a loud voice from heaven saying to them, 'Come up here.' And they ascended to heaven in a cloud, and their enemies saw them."

John's transport to heaven is a picture of the church being taken up to heaven before the tribulation begins.

The Saints Return with Christ

Some people doubt the rapture, but we must be in heaven during the tribulation to be able to return with Christ at the end of the tribulation.

> **Revelation 19:14**—"The armies in heaven, clothed in fine linen, white and clean, followed Him on white horses."

Those who follow Jesus back to Earth and are clothed in white are not angels, but believers.

> **Revelation 3:5**—"He who overcomes shall be clothed in white garments, and I will not blot out his name from the Book of Life; but I will confess his name before My Father and before His angels."
>
> **Jude 1:14-15**—"Now Enoch, the seventh from Adam, prophesied about these men also, saying, 'Behold, the Lord comes with ten thousands of His saints, to execute judgment on all, to convict all who are ungodly among them of all their ungodly deeds which they have committed in an ungodly way, and of all the harsh things which ungodly sinners have spoken against Him.'"
>
> **1 Thessalonians 3:12-13**—"May the Lord make you increase and abound in love to one another and to all, just as we do to you, so that He may establish your hearts blameless in holiness before our God and Father at the coming of our Lord Jesus Christ with all His saints."
>
> **1 Thessalonians 4:14**—"If we believe that Jesus died and rose again, even so God will bring with Him those who sleep in Jesus."

And consider how Paul comforted persecuted believers:

> **1 Thessalonians 5:2-11**—Though the day of the Lord comes as a "thief in the night," Paul says that "you, brethren, are not in darkness, so that this Day should overtake you as a thief,"

for "God did not appoint us to wrath, but to obtain salvation through our Lord Jesus Christ." He ends by asking us, in verse 11, to "comfort each other." However, what comfort is there in thinking that believers will experience the tribulation along with unbelievers? We therefore conclude that we will be absent from the earth during the tribulation.

The Hope of the Church

Paul, before he was martyred, wrote of longing for the appearing of Jesus.

> **2 Timothy 4:8**—"Finally, there is laid up for me the crown of righteousness, which the Lord, the righteous Judge, will give to me on that Day, and not to me only but also to all who have loved His appearing."

May we comfort each other with these words, longing for the Lord to call us home.

The Throne Room of Heaven

The Throne

> **Revelation 4:2**—"Immediately I was in the Spirit; and behold, a throne set in heaven, and One sat on the throne."

Fifteen times, the word "throne" is repeated in Revelation 4 and 5. And the "One" who sits on it is the Father, God Almighty.

The Appearance of God

> **REVELATION 4:3**–"He who sat there was like a jasper and a sardius stone in appearance; and there was a rainbow around the throne, in appearance like an emerald."

Jasper and sardius are reddish gemstones, and the rainbow around God's throne adds to the vision of the beautiful glow of God.

The 24 Elders

> **REVELATION 4:4a**—"Around the throne were twenty-four thrones, and on the thrones I saw twenty-four elders sitting, clothed in white robes."

Christians have debated the identity of the 24 elders:

- Some believe that 12 of the elders are the apostles, representing the church, and that the other 12 are the patriarchs, representing Israel. But that is unlikely because John would have mentioned himself as one of the elders sitting around the throne.
- Others conclude that the 24 elders represent the nation of Israel in general.

  1 Chronicles 24–25—God sorted the Levite priests and musicians in divisions of 24.

- Still others say this number simply represents the Old and New Testament saints, both Jewish and Gentile. This seems to be the best view.

Crowns of Gold

> **REVELATION 4:4b**—"I saw twenty-four elders sitting, clothed in white robes; and they had crowns of gold on their heads."

Here the word "crowns" is the Greek word *stephanos*. This refers to laurel-leaf crowns. These crowns will be given to show our victory in Christ.

But Jesus' "crown" in Revelation 6:2 is the Greek *diadéma*—a royal crown, a superior crown.

God's Throne

John's senses were bombarded with noise and colors coming from God's throne.

> **REVELATION 4:5a**—"From the throne proceeded lightnings, thunderings, and voices."

John saw before the throne the "seven Spirits," which probably refers to the fullness of the Spirit.

> **REVELATION 4:5b**—"Seven lamps of fire were burning before the throne, which are the seven Spirits of God."

We see also that "before the throne there was a sea of glass, like crystal" (Revelation 4:6a). But this sea is not literal. In the Bible, "sea" is often used figuratively, as in "the sea of humanity." But this sea is like glass, without waves troubling its surface, for it represents people who are at rest. Why? Because we are at rest in the presence of the Lord.

Four Living Creatures

These creatures have eyes on the back of their heads.

> **REVELATION 4:6b**—"In the midst of the throne, and around the throne, were four living creatures full of eyes in front and in back."

We read that these creatures are "like" four animals—they are not actually animals themselves. They are like a lion, a calf, a man, and an eagle. These creatures match the description of the four creatures in Ezekiel:

> **Ezekiel 1:5-21**—The prophet sees four creatures he describes as having the form of a man, the feet of a calf, the hands of a man, and each having four faces. The four faces are the face of man, a lion, an ox, and an eagle.

"Calf" can mean a baby ox, and if that is what John was referring to, then the creatures are the same as the ones Ezekiel saw. But Ezekiel saw them with four wings and John saw them with six. Isaiah 6 speaks of seraphim, which have six wings:

> **Isaiah 6:2**—"Above it stood seraphim; each one had six wings: with two he covered his face, with two he covered his feet, and with two he flew."

Taking these passages together, we can conclude that the creatures in Revelation 4 are cherubim or seraphim angels.

Holy, Holy, Holy

The angels in Revelation 4 have the job of praising the Lord, and they proclaim the holiness of the eternal God in triplets:

> **REVELATION 4:8b**—"They do not rest day or night, saying: 'Holy, holy, holy, Lord God Almighty, who was and is and is to come!'"

The triple praise emphasizes the perfection of God's holiness.

The Elders

> **REVELATION 4:9-10**—"Whenever the living creatures give glory and honor and thanks to Him who sits on the throne, who lives forever and ever, the twenty-four elders fall down before Him who sits on the throne and worship Him who lives forever and ever, and cast their crowns before the throne."

The elders worship along with the angels, casting their laurel crowns before the feet of the Lord. No one is self-aggrandizing here. Jesus gets all the glory.

Reflections on Revelation 4

Getting Started

In Revelation 4, John took us on a tour of the throne room of heaven, covering such sights as the majesty of the One True God, the 24 elders at his feet, and the angels around Him praising His holiness. Knowing that God's presence evokes such incredible wonder, we have to ask: What stops us from fixing our eyes on Him and worshipping Him constantly?

Study Questions

1. How does John indicate his transition to speaking about future events in Revelation 4:1 (see Revelation 1:19)? Why is it important to understand that there is a prophetic element to Revelation?
2. What are the three views on the timing of the rapture? Which view do you hold, and why?
3. How do the "door standing open in heaven," the voice "like a trumpet" (Revelation 4:1), and John's presence in heaven indicate that he is a picture of the raptured church (see 1 Corinthians 15:51-52; 2 Corinthians 5:8; 1 Thessalonians 4:16; Revelation 11:12; 19:11)?
4. First Thessalonians 4:18 tells us that the doctrine of the rapture should be comforting to us. How can we encourage each other with this hope (see 1 Thessalonians 5:2-11)?
5. In Revelation 19:14, an army in white garments returns with Christ at the end of the tribulation. Who makes up this army (1 Thessalonians 3:12-13; 4:14; Jude 1:14-15; Revelation 3:5), what attribute of God does this reveal, and why should this attribute comfort us (2 Corinthians 5:8)?

6. Review the description of God sitting on His throne. What does His appearance tell us about His nature and how we should relate to Him?
7. Who do the 24 elders represent, and what does that tell us about the makeup of heaven?
8. What is significant about John using different Greek words to describe the crowns of the elders (Revelation 4:4) and Jesus (Revelation 19:12)?
9. What does the sea still as glass before God's throne symbolize (Revelation 4:6)? How does this stillness encourage us to draw closer to Christ?
10. Why do the angels ascribe holiness to God three times in Revelation 4:8? How do you keep God's holiness in mind?

Important Takeaways for Us Today

1. Why do the elders throw crowns at the Lord's feet (Revelation 4:9-10)? Are you living in a way that would earn you a heavenly crown to adorn the feet of our Lord?
2. How does knowing that we can be raptured at any moment compel you to live for Christ and share the gospel?

5

Behold, the Lamb

REVELATION 5

Who is worthy to reveal the end of all things? In Revelation 5, when an angel asks this very question, no one is found worthy in heaven above or on Earth below to unseal the scroll of the prophecy until Jesus, the Lion of Judah and Lamb of God, steps up to open the scroll. And to this great Savior, every nation and tongue bows in worship, for He alone is worthy to open the seals and commence the judgment of the world.

The Lamb Takes the Scroll

The Scroll

God is spirit, but He showed Himself to John in a physical representation. God was holding a scroll in His right hand. This scroll has so much written on it that the words cover both the front and back. And God gave this scroll, which is the title deed to Earth, to Jesus the Son. God is not finished with those on Earth, and He will use each judgment that the Son pronounces as final wake-up calls to draw people to the saving knowledge of Christ.

The Seven Seals

The seven seals must be opened before the scroll can be "read"; that is, the events of the seven seals must come to pass before what's in the scroll can occur.

But no one in all the earth was worthy to open the scroll—until Christ stepped forward.

Names of God

The Lion of the Tribe of Judah, the Root of David

John referred to Jesus as "the Lion of the tribe of Judah, the Root of David" (Revelation 5:5). This is a messianic title referenced as far back as Genesis. When the patriarch Jacob was near death, he prophesied that the Messiah King would come from the tribe of Judah.

> **Genesis 49:9-10**—"Judah is a lion's whelp; from the prey, my son, you have gone up. He bows down, he lies down as a lion; and as a lion, who shall rouse him? The scepter shall not depart from Judah, nor a lawgiver from between his feet, until Shiloh comes; and to Him shall be the obedience of the people."

Jacob's prediction is fulfilled in Christ, the Lion of Judah.

Isaiah also prophesied about the Messiah coming from Judah, and from Jesse specifically.

> **Isaiah 11:10**—"In that day there shall be a Root of Jesse, who shall stand as a banner to the people; for the Gentiles shall seek Him, And His resting place shall be glorious."

John's prophecy is more specific, calling Jesus the "Root of David," who is the son of Jesse, of the tribe of Judah.

> **REVELATION 5:5**–"One of the elders said to me, 'Do not weep. Behold, the Lion of the tribe of Judah, the Root of David, has prevailed to open the scroll and to loose its seven seals.'"

The Lamb

> **REVELATION 5:6a**–"I looked, and behold, in the midst of the throne and of the four living creatures, and in the midst of the elders, stood a Lamb as though it had been slain."

Jesus prefers His redemptive title of "Lamb" over any other, and this will be the only title, used 19 times, to describe Him throughout the rest of Revelation.

Revelation 1–4 emphasizes the majesty of Jesus, but from chapter 5 on, we see a focus on Jesus' sacrificial service.

In the Old Testament, an innocent lamb could be slain to assuage a sinner's guilty conscience, and foreshadowed the atonement to come. In the New Testament, Jesus came as the Lamb of God who takes away the sins of people, once for all, fulfilling the Old Testament sacrificial system by His sacrifice on the cross.

> **John 1:29**—"The next day John [the Baptist] saw Jesus coming toward him, and said, 'Behold! The Lamb of God who takes away the sin of the world!'"

And Paul also called on Jesus' redemptive title in his letter to the Corinthians.

> **1 Corinthians 5:7b (ESV)**—"Christ, our Passover lamb, has been sacrificed."

It has been said that the only man-made things in heaven are the marks on Jesus' hands and feet, the Lamb of God crucified for us.

Seven Horns, Seven Eyes

> **REVELATION 5:6b**–John then saw a lamb "having seven horns and seven eyes, which are the seven Spirits of God sent out into all the earth."

The number seven symbolizes perfection, horns symbolize power, and eyes symbolize wisdom and knowledge. This paints a picture of Jesus as the all-powerful, all-wise, all-knowing God.

And this perfect God takes the scroll.

Worthy Is the Lamb

Harps and Bowls

> **REVELATION 5:8**–"Now when He had taken the scroll, the four living creatures and the twenty-four elders fell down before the Lamb, each having a harp, and golden bowls full of incense, which are the prayers of the saints."

Here, John mentioned harps, though most likely what this passage describes is closer to zithers, another kind of stringed instrument. Either way, musical worship is a major aspect of all that takes place in heaven.

But there is also the worship of our words: the golden bowls filled with our prayers.

> **Psalm 141:2**—"Let my prayer be set before You as incense, the lifting up of my hands as the evening sacrifice."

How amazing it is to know that God loves to hear us—that our prayers are preserved and none of our cries go unnoticed by our Lord.

In the Old Testament, the priests would light incense as a picture of our prayers rising to God. Remember, your prayers are noted, heard, and recorded. Regardless of how God answers, He hears.

Every Nation

> **REVELATION 5:9b**–"You are worthy to take the scroll, and to open its seals; for You were slain, and have redeemed us to God by Your blood out of every tribe and tongue and people and nation.'"

Heaven will be filled with diverse people and cultures. There will be no segregation in heaven! We will all be worshipping around the throne of God regardless of ethnicity, race, or nationality. Believers will be one people, with one tongue, worshipping one Lord!

Kings and Priests

> **REVELATION 5:10**—"And have made us kings and priests to our God; and we shall reign on the earth."

During the millennium, we will reign with Christ on the earth.

Choir of Praise

> **REVELATION 5:11-12**—"I looked, and I heard the voice of many angels around the throne, the living creatures, and the elders; and the number of them was ten thousand times ten thousand, and thousands of thousands, saying with a loud voice:
>
> "Worthy is the Lamb who was slain to receive power and riches and wisdom, and strength and honor and glory and blessing!"

This large number is probably not literal, but figurative, meant to illustrate that the number of saints will be innumerable.

And they are not alone in their worship.

> **REVELATION 5:13**—"Every creature which is in heaven and on the earth and under the earth and such as are in the sea, and all that are in them, I heard saying: 'Blessing and honor and glory and power be to Him who sits on the throne, and to the Lamb, forever and ever!'"

Every creature, great and small, will worship the Creator. Imagine that!

Reflections on Revelation 5

Getting Started

Before God revealed His judgments, He established who Jesus is and how we as the saints are to respond to the knowledge of Him. Similarly, we can be changed daily as we learn more about Jesus in His Word. While reading through Revelation 5, which of Jesus' titles stood out to you and what response does this name for Jesus evoke?

Study Questions

1. What is God's purpose with each judgment, and how can we take part in acting out God's purposes today?
2. What does the scroll with seven seals symbolize (Revelation 5:1)? And why is it significant that only Jesus can open this sealed scroll (see Deuteronomy 10:14; Job 41:11; Psalm 24:1)?
3. In Revelation 5:5, Jesus is called "the Lion of the tribe of Judah" and "the Root of David." What roles does this title ascribe to Jesus (see Genesis 49:9-10; Isaiah 11:10), and how should we respond (see Deuteronomy 18:18-19)?
4. What is the significance of the reference to Jesus as "the Lamb" in Revelation 5:6? How does Jesus' sacrifice affect how you live (see 2 Corinthians 5:15)?
5. Some say that the only man-made things in heaven are the wounds Jesus bears. Why would Jesus keep these marks? How should you honor Jesus' sacrifice (see Romans 12:1-2)?
6. In Revelation 5:6, why is Jesus described as the Lamb with seven horns and seven eyes? How are these attributes of God pertinent to end-times events (see Romans 11:33-36)?
7. What is the significance of the golden bowls full of incense

mentioned in Revelation 5:8 (see Psalm 141:2)? How should this comfort us?

8. What does the composition of heaven tell us about God's love (Revelation 5:9) and how we should behave toward our fellow man?
9. Who makes up the choir praising God in Revelation 5:11-13? How does this illuminate the purpose of creation (see Romans 11:36)?

Important Takeaways for Us Today

1. The harps, or zithers, in heaven show us God's view on the importance of worship (Revelation 5:8). What are some ways you prioritize worship in your life?
2. One of the songs of praise the saints sing to the Lord is in Revelation 5:10, sung in gratitude for God's choice to appoint believers as "kings and priests to our God." What is involved in these roles, and how should we fulfill them (see 1 Peter 2:9)?

6

The Beginning of the End

REVELATION 6

Imagine a quarter of the world's population vanishing. What would happen to our labor force? To our ability to produce food? To innovate? To create wealth? The effects of the rapture will be massive, and in this vacuum, the Antichrist will rise. And his arrival is only the first seal judgment. Six more will follow.

Six Seal Judgments

Context

The Lamb takes the scroll and opens the seven seals (Revelation 5:1-5), and the judgments begin, starting with the seal judgments, then the trumpet judgments, then the bowl (or vial) judgments. All of this is God's attempt to get men to repent before the final judgment.

May these passages motivate us to share the gospel with our unsaved friends and loved ones because we do not know how much time is left. But when the tribulation comes, life on Earth will be catastrophic.

First Seal

Jesus opens the first seal, and in comes a man on a white horse.

> **REVELATION 6:1-2**—"Now I saw when the Lamb opened one of the seals; and I heard one of the four living creatures saying with a voice like thunder, 'Come and see.' And I looked, and behold, a white horse. He who sat on it had a bow; and a crown was given to him, and he went out conquering and to conquer."

This man is not Jesus. This man is part of the first judgment and is described as coming with a bow without arrows, which symbolizes peace. The missing arrows tells us that for the moment, the rider's intent is hidden. But though he has come under the guise of peace, war is in his heart.

The rider of the white horse also wears a crown, but this is not a *diadéma* crown like the royal crown Jesus wears. This is *stephanos*, a laurel-wreath crown. What this rider wears is an inferior, perishable crown, signifying he is allowed to rule for a season.

Antichrist

The rider of the white horse is none other than the Antichrist. The Antichrist has many titles throughout the Bible:

1. The man of lawlessness, or the lawless one

> **2 Thessalonians 2:8**—"The lawless one will be revealed, whom the Lord will consume with the breath of His mouth and destroy with the brightness of His coming."

2. The abomination that causes desolation

> **Matthew 24:15**—"When you see the 'abomination of desolation,' spoken of by Daniel the prophet, standing in the holy place…"

Jesus referred to the "abomination that causes desolation," spoken of by Daniel, as being a future event. The Antichrist will fulfill this prophecy, proclaiming himself to be God (2 Thessalonians 2:4).

> **Daniel 9:27**—"He shall confirm a covenant with many for one week; but in the middle of the week he shall bring an end to sacrifice and offering. And on the wing of abominations shall be one who makes desolate, even until the consummation, which is determined, is poured out on the desolate."

An Antichrist

Daniel spoke prophetically with a dual application. The near interpretation of this prophecy has to do with a prideful Greek king by the name of Antiochus IV, who mistreated the Jews in many ways. This king, who ruled over the Seleucid Empire (175–164 BC), arrogantly gave himself the additional title *Epiphanes*, which means "the presence of God," because that was how he viewed himself.

This Antiochus was rebuffed by an Egyptian king, so in 168 BC, he showed his displeasure by murdering many Jews. Then he slaughtered a pig in the temple of God as a gesture of blatant disregard for the Jews and the God of Israel. This was the "abomination that causes desolation."

Maccabean Revolt

In response to this abomination, Judas Maccabeus led a Jewish uprising called the Maccabean Revolt. His forces took back the temple and purged it of the desolation.

The Antichrist

Prophecy tells us this Antichrist will blaspheme God's temple by setting himself up in the temple and proclaiming himself to be God (2 Thessalonians 2:4). There has not been a Jewish temple standing on the Temple Mount of Jerusalem since it was destroyed in AD 70 by the Roman Emperor Titus Vespasian, which means that a temple must be built at some point in the future. This building effort will cause many

Jews who do not believe that Jesus is the Messiah to put their faith in the Antichrist, presuming him to be the Messiah instead. They will put their faith in this Antichrist until he commits the abomination of desolation.

3. The man of sin, the son of perdition

> **2 Thessalonians 2:3**—"Let no one deceive you by any means; for that Day will not come unless the falling away comes first, and the man of sin is revealed, the son of perdition."

The Antichrist comes after a great falling away.

The Bible portrays the Antichrist as a charismatic political figure who will secure peace in the Middle East. He will, no doubt, secure peace between Muslims, Jews, and Christians concerning the Temple Mount—a feat others have tried to accomplish yet failed. President Bill Clinton came close to brokering a peace deal regarding the Temple Mount between the Palestine Liberation Organization leader at the time (Yasser Arafat) and the prime minister of Israel at the time (Ehud Barak). But Arafat did not agree with the terms, even though he was offered more than 90 percent of what he asked for.

Many Jews who currently do not believe Jesus is the Messiah will fall for the Antichrist. Not until halfway through the seven-year peace treaty will the Antichrist reveal who he really is, and they will then realize they have been deceived.

4. The foolish shepherd

> **Zechariah 11:15-16**—"The Lord said to me, 'Next, take for yourself the implements of a foolish shepherd. For indeed I will raise up a shepherd in the land who will not care for those who are cut off, nor seek the young, nor heal those that are broken, nor feed those that still stand. But he will eat the flesh of the fat and tear their hooves in pieces.'"

5. The king who exalts himself

> **Daniel 11:36-39**—"The king shall do according to his own will: he shall exalt and magnify himself above every god, shall speak blasphemies against the God of gods, and shall prosper till the wrath has been accomplished; for what has been determined shall be done. He shall regard neither the God of his fathers nor the desire of women, nor regard any god; for he shall exalt himself above them all. But in their place he shall honor a god of fortresses; and a god which his fathers did not know he shall honor with gold and silver, with precious stones and pleasant things. Thus he shall act against the strongest fortresses with a foreign god, which he shall acknowledge, and advance its glory; and he shall cause them to rule over many, and divide the land for gain."

But the Antichrist's reign will be short:

> **Revelation 19:20**—"The beast was captured, and with him the false prophet who worked signs in his presence, by which he deceived those who received the mark of the beast and those who worshiped his image. These two were cast alive into the lake of fire burning with brimstone."

Even now, there could be a government leader who will rise to fill the role of Antichrist, but hopefully we are out of here before we get the opportunity to meet him!

Second Seal

> **REVELATION 6:3-4**–"When He opened the second seal, I heard the second living creature saying, 'Come and see.' Another horse, fiery red, went out. And it was granted to the one who sat on it to take peace from the earth, and that people should kill one another; and there was given to him a great sword."

The rider on the red horse comes as the second seal is opened, and because red is the color of terror and bloodshed, and the sword that the rider carries symbolizes war, God is symbolically telling us that great war will come upon the earth.

Third Seal

At the heels of the war will come a great economic collapse.

> **REVELATION 6:5-6**—"When He opened the third seal, I heard the third living creature say, 'Come and see.' So I looked, and behold, a black horse, and he who sat on it had a pair of scales in his hand. And I heard a voice in the midst of the four living creatures saying, 'A quart of wheat for a denarius, and three quarts of barley for a denarius; and do not harm the oil and the wine.'"

Jesus opens the third seal and in comes the rider on the black horse, who represents famine and economic collapse.

Economic collapse means rising food prices. A "quart of wheat" is the measure necessary to make a loaf of bread, and a "denarius" is a day's wage, meaning that the cost of a loaf of bread would be, in today's currency, about $200.

Think of how COVID shut down the world, leading to businesses closing and higher unemployment rates. Now take that further and consider what the previous seal was and how all the countries are economically connected today. Any country's economic collapse can have a domino effect around the world.

In 2021, as many as 828 million people were labeled as "food insecure" by the United Nations.[1] The global economy is fragile. It will not take much to send the world into a famine.

Fourth Seal

> **REVELATION 6:7-8**—"When He opened the fourth seal, I heard the voice of the fourth living creature saying, 'Come and see.' So I looked, and behold, a pale horse. And the name of him who sat on it was Death, and Hades followed with him. And power was given to them over a fourth of the earth, to kill with sword, with hunger, with death, and by the beasts of the earth."

The rider on the pale horse arrives. "Pale" in the Greek text is *chlōros*, which is where we get our word *chlorophyll*, meaning that "pale" here refers to a pale green color.

This rider and his horse represent the death of many unbelievers through war, famine, plague, and wild beasts. The fourth seal brings the death of more than a quarter of Earth's population. To better picture the magnitude of this, imagine the loss of 2 billion out of the 7.9 billion people on Earth.

And consider how devastating plagues can be: Many tens of millions of people died during World War II, and there were many more deaths after the war because the unsanitary conditions of the battlefields brought on influenza and typhoid. And the bubonic plague, also known as the black death, killed an estimated 30 to 50 percent of Europe's population during the fourteenth century. That was an estimated 75 million to 200 million people.[2]

Fifth Seal

Then believers are persecuted to death.

> **REVELATION 6:9-11**—"When He opened the fifth seal, I saw under the altar the souls of those who had been slain for the word of God and for the testimony which they held. And they cried with a loud voice, saying, 'How long, O Lord, holy

> and true, until You judge and avenge our blood on those who dwell on the earth?' Then a white robe was given to each of them; and it was said to them that they should rest a little while longer, until both the number of their fellow servants and their brethren, who would be killed as they were, was completed."

These individuals are martyred for not worshipping the beast or receiving his mark (Revelation 13:15). Remember, those who were not raptured can still get saved during the tribulation. They will have woken up to the truth of God because of one of His judgments. The saints who are killed during the tribulation will cry out to God to avenge their murders, but God will tell them to wait, for there will be more martyrs before the end comes.

Sixth Seal

The sixth seal unleashes universal natural catastrophes.

> **REVELATION 6:12-13**–"I looked when He opened the sixth seal, and behold, there was a great earthquake; and the sun became black as sackcloth of hair, and the moon became like blood. And the stars of heaven fell to the earth, as a fig tree drops its late figs when it is shaken by a mighty wind."

Natural calamities can have an enormous effect on surrounding areas. In 1883, Krakatoa erupted. The eruption was heard 3,000 miles away, it created tidal waves 1,500 miles away, and it changed the tides for 1,700 miles. The eruption of one volcano changed the globe's weather for two years. Imagine what these global disasters will do to Earth.

Everything is already set for what is to come. An article in *Science Advances* says the moon is rusting, leaving scientists perplexed.[3] Lead article writer Shuai Li of the University of Hawaii said, "It's very puzzling." The moon is a terrible environment for the formation of hematite—hematite being the iron mineral that makes Mars red—but nevertheless, it is forming and rusting the moon. Besides this, there are more than 18 thousand NEOs, or near-Earth objects, that could careen into Earth at any moment.

The world will become undone, and conditions will become so unbearable that people wish for death.

> **REVELATION 6:14-17**—"Then the sky receded as a scroll when it is rolled up, and every mountain and island was moved out of its place. And the kings of the earth, the great men, the rich men, the commanders, the mighty men, every slave and every free man, hid themselves in the caves and in the rocks of the mountains, and said to the mountains and rocks, 'Fall on us and hide us from the face of Him who sits on the throne and from the wrath of the Lamb! For the great day of His wrath has come, and who is able to stand?'"

Unfortunately, many will choose to hide from God rather than turn to Him.

Reflections on Revelation 6

Getting Started

Revelation 6 covers the first six seals, showing the world quickly going from bad to worse. Why do you think the world will self-destruct so quickly (see Jeremiah 12:17; Romans 1:28; Galatians 6:7), and how should we live in light of this truth (see 2 Chronicles 7:14; Psalm 33:12; Proverbs 1:7)?

Study Questions

1. How should knowing that Christ can come at any moment change how we see the world?
2. When Antichrist comes, he will pretend to be a man of peace (Revelation 6:2). What does this tell us about the nature of evil (2 Corinthians 11:14)?
3. Why does Jesus call the Antichrist "the abomination that causes desolation" in Matthew 24:15 when Daniel used this title to reference Antiochus IV in Daniel 9:27 (see 1 John 2:18)? Why is this important for us to know (see 2 Thessalonians 2:3)?
4. The Antichrist is called the foolish shepherd (Zechariah 11:15-16) in contrast to Christ's title as the Good Shepherd (John 10:11). What are the contrasting attributes these titles evoke, and how are we to mimic our Good Shepherd's example (see Ephesians 5:2; Hebrews 13:15-16)?
5. What seal judgment immediately follows the first rider despite his promise of peace (Revelation 6:3-4)? How can you protect yourself against the enemy's deception (see 2 Timothy 3:13-17)?

6. How are the second (Revelation 6:3-4), third (verses 5-6), and fourth (verses 7-8) seals related? How does the fragility of life point us to how we should live (see James 4:13-15)?
7. Why will God allow tribulation Christians to die for the faith (Revelation 6:9-11)? What does this reflect about God's character (see 2 Peter 3:9)?
8. At the fifth seal judgment, Christian martyrs will cry out for God to avenge them (Revelation 6:9-11). How does God answer them? How does this inform our understanding of justice (see Psalm 73:3-22, 27)?
9. How is the world already set up for the sixth seal judgment (Revelation 6:12-13)? How should we respond to knowing that the world itself will one day unravel, beginning with the seal judgments, and then later, in a moment (see 2 Peter 3:10-13)?
10. Why will people hide from God rather than run to Him when the tribulation strikes (Revelation 6:14-17)?

Important Takeaways for Us Today

1. Note that one title for the Antichrist is "the king who exalts himself" (Daniel 11:36-39). What does this tell us about God's view of pride? In what areas of your life has God convicted you of pride, and what kind of change do you think He desires?
2. Revelation 6:15 remarks how men from various stations will be brought low, and verse 17 ends with the question of who will be able to stand. What allows a person to stand in that Day (see Revelation 7:2-3), and how does that move you to gratitude?

7

The Remnant

REVELATION 7

Do you ever need a break from watching the news? That is what happens in Revelation chapter 7. Between the sixth and seventh seal judgments, God gives us an intermission to comfort us about the wrath to come. Remember, Revelation was written amid a time of great persecution, and for the Christians of that time, chapter 7 was a gleam of hope: a light in the darkness of their world. Let us celebrate as they did that Jesus will always keep to Himself a remnant "whose knees have not bowed to Baal" (1 Kings 19:18).

The Context

Reasons for Tribulation

1. To wake up unbelievers—their window of opportunity to repent will soon close.
2. To shake up Israel—God is not done with the Jewish people.
3. To build up the kingdom of God—there will not be endless opportunities for the lost to get saved. There will come a time when there is no more opportunity.

An Intermission

John did not immediately move on to the seventh seal judgment. He does not bring it up until chapter 8, and the opening of the seventh seal heralds the seven trumpet judgments. In chapter 7, we are given a behind-the-scenes glimpse of what's happening with the saints.

This is because chapter 6 ends with an ominous note.

> Revelation 6:17—"For the great day of His wrath has come, and who is able to stand?"

Answer? The remnant. They will stand.

The Two Visions

I Saw

John had two visions. The first is described in verses 1 to 8, beginning with the phrase "I saw."

> **REVELATION 7:1**—"After these things I saw four angels standing at the four corners of the earth, holding the four winds of the earth, that the wind should not blow on the earth, on the sea, or on any tree."

I Looked

The second is given in verses 9 to 17, beginning with the phrase "I looked."

> **REVELATION 7:9**—"After these things I looked, and behold, a great multitude which no one could number, of all nations, tribes, peoples, and tongues, standing before the throne and before the Lamb, clothed with white robes, with palm branches in their hands."

Both phrases, "I saw" and "I looked," use the same Greek verb.

The Sealed

Four Angels

In Revelation 7:1, John said that four angels will stand at the "four corners of the earth" not because the Bible denies that the world is round, but because he was using an idiom, similar to when we talk about the four points of a compass.

And the four angels are standing in positions of judgment. They are told to withhold the wind, that "the wind should not blow on the earth" (Revelation 7:1). In biblical typology, "wind" is an indication of judgment, so this is probably not literal wind, but a reference to judgment.

The Fifth Angel

There is a fifth angel given power over the other four.

> **REVELATION 7:2a**–"Then I saw another angel ascending from the east, having the seal of the living God."

Some believe this angel is Jesus, but I would disagree because the Greek phrase translated "another angel" here is *allos angelos*, meaning "an angel of the same kind."

But the fifth angel does have more authority than the other four. This is not unusual, for the Bible tells us that both good and fallen angels are separated into ranks.

> **Ephesians 6:12**—"We do not wrestle against flesh and blood, but against principalities, against powers, against the rulers of the darkness of this age, against spiritual hosts of wickedness in the heavenly places."

Also, Gabriel was a messenger angel, Michael was an archangel, and Lucifer had a high rank before God cast him out of heaven due to his pride.

> **REVELATION 7:2b-3**—"He [the fifth angel] cried with a loud voice to the four angels to whom it was granted to harm the earth and the sea, saying, 'Do not harm the earth, the sea, or the trees till we have sealed the servants of our God on their foreheads.'"

It is not unusual that though the four angels have God-given authority to execute judgment on Earth, the fifth angel has the authority to restrain them. Ultimately, all are following God's command to withhold judgment till He can seal His people.

The 144,000

The servants are numbered here at 144,000. The Bible does not describe what the sealed will look like but does say God will use them to do remarkable things. And because parts of Revelation are not in chronological order, we will read more about these evangelists in Revelation chapter 14.

Who are these 144,000? First, let's look at who they will not be. Jehovah's Witnesses say they are the 144,000, but there are nine million Jehovah's Witnesses in the world.[1]

Then who are they? Revelation tells us: They are Jews who will come to Christ during the tribulation. God will pick 12,000 from each tribe of Israel.

> **REVELATION 7:4-8**—"I heard the number of those who were sealed. One hundred and forty-four thousand of all the tribes of the children of Israel were sealed:
>
> > "of the tribe of Judah twelve thousand were sealed; of the tribe of Reuben twelve thousand were sealed; of the tribe of Gad twelve thousand were sealed; of the tribe of Asher twelve thousand were sealed; of the tribe of Naphtali twelve thousand were sealed; of the tribe of Manasseh twelve thousand were sealed; of the tribe of Simeon twelve thousand were sealed; of the tribe of Levi twelve

> thousand were sealed; of the tribe of Issachar twelve thousand were sealed; of the tribe of Zebulun twelve thousand were sealed; of the tribe of Joseph twelve thousand were sealed; of the tribe of Benjamin twelve thousand were sealed."

The 144,000 will be

1. sealed on their foreheads
2. servants of God
3. from each of the 12 tribes of Israel

Levi

The 12 tribes come from the twelve sons of Jacob, whom God renamed Israel. But it is unusual for Levi to be included in the list because unlike the other tribes, God gave the Levites a special inheritance as His priests, which means they are not often numbered alongside the other tribes.

However, in this list, God mentions Levi, but not the tribe of Dan.

Dan

Some believe that the Antichrist will come from the tribe of Dan, pointing to when Jacob blessed his 12 sons before he died, saying a blessing over Judah but a curse upon Dan:

> **Genesis 49:10**—"The scepter shall not depart from Judah, nor a lawgiver from between his feet, until Shiloh comes; and to Him shall be the obedience of the people." This prophesized the Messiah would come from Judah.

> **Genesis 49:17**—"Dan shall be a serpent by the way, a viper by the path, that bites the horse's heels so that its rider shall fall backward." This could prophesy that the Antichrist will come from Dan.

But others believe that the Antichrist will be the Pope, or perhaps a Muslim.

Still, even though the tribe of Dan is not mentioned in Revelation 7, God has not forgotten or discarded them. The tribe of Dan reappears in the future and is listed among the tribes of Israel during the millennial period (see Ezekiel 48:1-2, 32).

Joseph

Joseph is mentioned in Revelation 7:8, and that, too, is unusual because he received a double portion of blessing, and his two sons—Manasseh and Ephraim—are usually inserted in place of their father when the tribes are mentioned. Yet while Manasseh is mentioned in verse 6, Ephraim is omitted, with Joseph listed instead.

Some believe this is because during Israel's worst days of idolatry, Dan and Ephraim were both given to idolatry and even had temples consecrated to idols. So perhaps they are not represented because of their idolatry, but again, they both also come back during the millennium.

The Genealogy of the 12

There are no delineations between the Jewish people anymore. Unless you are a Jew with a surname like Levi or Cohen, meaning "Levite" or "priest," Jews today typically do not know which tribe they belong to. The Assyrian invasion, the Babylonian invasion, and the Roman conquest destroyed all records, and had there been anything left, the Nazi Holocaust would have destroyed any trace of Jewish records of tribal identity, *but God knows everything*! He does not need human records to know the tribal identity of every Jew in the world.

The Multitude

The Gentiles

The second vision begins with Gentile believers praising God.

REVELATION 7:9—"After these things I looked, and behold, a great multitude which no one could number, of all nations, tribes, peoples, and tongues, standing before the throne and before the Lamb, clothed with white robes, with palm branches in their hands."

There are too many believers to count. They are wearing white robes as a sign of purity, and they hold palm branches in their hands, reminiscent of when worshippers lined the road to Jerusalem on Palm Sunday, waving palm branches as Jesus arrived for the final week of His life.

> **John 12:13**—The people "took branches of palm trees and went out to meet Him, and cried out: 'Hosanna! "Blessed is He who comes in the name of the Lord!" The King of Israel!'"

The palm branches are signs of victory and of worship for their King, which they present to Him along with this cry:

REVELATION 7:10—The saints were "crying out with a loud voice, saying, 'Salvation belongs to our God who sits on the throne, and to the Lamb!'"

The Heavenly Scene

The tribulation saints were not alone in their worship.

REVELATION 7:11-12—"All the angels stood around the throne and the elders and the four living creatures, and fell on their faces before the throne and worshiped God, saying:

> "Amen! Blessing and glory and wisdom, Thanksgiving and honor and power and might, Be to our God forever and ever. Amen."

All the angels, however many there are in heaven, will surround the throne of God with their worship. The four living creatures, as part of the angelic choir, will join in the worship. The elders, the same 24 elders of Revelation 4, will praise God, representing the Old Testament believers and the New Testament church.

Heaven is about worship. We are not going to be in God's presence with our list of questions. We are going to be flat on our faces, humble before God!

White Robes

An unnamed elder answered a question John was perhaps too overwhelmed to ask.

> **REVELATION 7:13-14**—"One of the elders answered, saying to me, 'Who are these arrayed in white robes, and where did they come from?'
>
> "And I said to him, 'Sir, you know.'
>
> "So he said to me, 'These are the ones who come out of the great tribulation, and washed their robes and made them white in the blood of the Lamb.'"

The saints in white robes are those martyred for Christ during the tribulation. Notice their robes are not red, despite how the elder says they were washed in Christ's blood. That is a reference to Christ's death on the cross, and how God's righteousness is appropriated to His saints.

Also, "robes" in the Greek text is *stole*, which is where we get our English word *stole*, meaning "a long flowing garment." And "white" in the Greek is *leukainō*, from the root word *leukos*, meaning "light." So, these long garments are glowing as a reflection of God's glory upon them.

These tribulation saints serve God at His temple, and they, along with those who were dead in Christ, will return with the Lord, ruling and reigning with Him:

REVELATION 7:15–"Therefore they are before the throne of God and serve Him day and night in His temple. And He who sits on the throne will dwell among them."

This passage reminds us that amid God's wrath, He shows mercy. And what a wonderful way to end this chapter: with the comfort of the Lord. Though in this life we may suffer, when we stand in His presence, we will know that what we endured was worth it.

REVELATION 7:16-17–"They shall neither hunger anymore nor thirst anymore; the sun shall not strike them, nor any heat; for the Lamb who is in the midst of the throne will shepherd them and lead them to living fountains of waters. And God will wipe away every tear from their eyes."

Romans 8:18—"I consider that the sufferings of this present time are not worthy to be compared with the glory which shall be revealed in us."

Reflections on Revelation 7

Getting Started

Amid Jesus' judgment on Earth, God showed John two visions of His people, and the latter one was about heaven's population worshipping Jesus as the Lamb of God who saved them. How is this contrast of God's justice and judgment and His mercy and salvation still consistent with the nature of Christ (see Exodus 34:6-7; Psalm 85:10; Romans 2:7-11)?

Study Questions

1. There is an intermission between the sixth and seventh seal judgments because Revelation 7 is written to answer a question. What is the question and the answer (see Revelation 6:17)? Why is this answer comforting (see 2 Peter 2:9)?
2. What phrases did John use to introduce two separate visions (Revelation 7:1, 9)? How do these two visions (Revelation 7:1-8, 9-17) complement each other and illustrate two different ways to stand during the tribulation (see Daniel 3:17-18; Hebrews 11:32-39)?
3. In Revelation 7:2-3, John spoke of a fifth angel who had authority over the previous four, and some believe this angel is Jesus. How do we know that he is not (see Hebrews 1:4)?
4. Why is it notable that God withholds judgment till 144,000 of his servants are sealed, according to Revelation 7:3 (see Romans 11:2-5)?
5. Jehovah's Witnesses believe they are the 144,000, but why is this not possible? Who will make up the 144,000 (Revelation 7:4-8)?

6. Why is the tribe of Dan likely not included among the Jews sealed by God (see Genesis 49:10, 17)? What does the later restoration of Dan (see Ezekiel 48:1-2, 32) tell us about God (see Joel 2:13)?
7. Why is today's lack of tribal delineations between Jews irrelevant to the prophecy of the 144,000?
8. In Revelation 7:9, John described the saints coming to Jesus with palm branches. What do the palm branches reference (see John 12:13), and how do we praise Jesus as King with our lives?
9. The men arrayed in white and praising God are those martyred for the faith (Revelation 7:13-14). How can we take comfort from this scene (see Revelation 7:16-17; Romans 8:18)?
10. John described the saints' robes as "white" with the Greek word *leukainō* (Revelation 7:14). What does this word tell us about how God sees us?

Important Takeaways for Us Today

1. Jesus has already washed us clean (Revelation 7:14), but He calls us to walk in that truth. How do you fix your gaze on Jesus and not grow weary in well doing (see Romans 12:2; Galatians 5:16-17; 6:9; 2 Timothy 3:16)?
2. God calls us to follow Him even when it costs us (Revelation 7:13-17). What gives you the courage to follow Christ when those around you are calling you to go a different way (Romans 8:18; 2 Corinthians 10:5; 2 Timothy 1:7)?

8

The Calm and the Storm

REVELATION 8

Have you ever seen a loud crowd suddenly fall silent? There is a certain level of fear born in unnatural silences. We see this kind of foreboding in Revelation chapter 8 when heaven goes from every creature praising God to immediate and prolonged silence for the space of "half an hour" (Revelation 8:1). This is the calm before the storm—the storm of four of the seven trumpet judgments that fall upon the earth. Then another sort of fearful expectation comes, for at the end of this chapter, an angel warns that there are more judgments ahead.

Prelude to the Trumpets

Seventh Seal

Back to the end of the world.

> **REVELATION 8:1a**–"When He opened the seventh seal..."

Jesus opening the seventh seal leads to the seven trumpet judgments.

Half an Hour

> **REVELATION 8:1b**–"…there was silence in heaven for about half an hour."

The angels, living creatures, elders, and martyrs had just been praising God, but now there is a pregnant pause, and it is very foreboding.

Seven Trumpets

Seven Angels

God entrusts "the" seven angels with seven trumpets.

> **REVELATION 8:2**–"I saw the seven angels who stand before God, and to them were given seven trumpets."

John's use of the direct article "the" indicates the seven are specific angels dispatched for a purpose.

Another Angel

> **REVELATION 8:3a**–"Then another angel, having a golden censer, came and stood at the altar."

Some believe this eighth angel to be Jesus because of the priestly role he takes on by connecting man to God and God to man. But even human beings served in a priestly role, as mentioned in Leviticus.

Also, the word "another" is *allos* in the Greek text, which means "one of the same kind." Thus, this is an angel like the other seven.

The Saints' Prayers

God hears His people. In heaven, there is a "golden censer" containing all the saints' prayers to God.

> **REVELATION 8:3**—"Another angel, having a golden censer, came and stood at the altar. He was given much incense, that he should offer it with the prayers of all the saints upon the golden altar which was before the throne."

This talk of an altar and incense harkens back to the temple plans God gave to Moses and then David—a temple that Solomon later built. The earthly temple was to be a picture for us of the temple God has in heaven.

> **Hebrews 8:5**—The earthly priests are those "who serve the copy and shadow of the heavenly things, as Moses was divinely instructed when he was about to make the tabernacle. For He said, 'See that you make all things according to the pattern shown you on the mountain.'"

And as the prayers of the saints go up, the judgments come down:

> **REVELATION 8:4-5**—"The smoke of the incense, with the prayers of the saints, ascended before God from the angel's hand. Then the angel took the censer, filled it with fire from the altar, and threw it to the earth. And there were noises, thunderings, lightnings, and an earthquake."

At these noises, the angels ready their positions to execute the trumpet judgments.

> **REVELATION 8:6**—"The seven angels who had the seven trumpets prepared themselves to sound."

First Trumpet

> **REVELATION 8:7**—"The first angel sounded: And hail and fire followed, mingled with blood, and they were thrown to the earth. And a third of the trees were burned up, and all green grass was burned up."

The phrase "mingled with blood" probably refers to the many people who will die at the first trumpet announcing hail and fire.

But they will also die because these judgments will have a domino effect. Without green grass, livestock will suffer and die. Without livestock, food supplies for people will be greatly reduced.

The environmental movement has become a religion of its own, with people worshipping creation over the Creator (Romans 1:25). But while we ought to be good stewards of what God has given us, it will all burn anyway (2 Peter 3). The tree huggers will have conniptions. The environmentalists will need therapy. All this world is going to burn!

Second Trumpet

> **REVELATION 8:8-9**—"The second angel sounded: And something like a great mountain burning with fire was thrown into the sea, and a third of the sea became blood. And a third of the living creatures in the sea died, and a third of the ships were destroyed."

Remember John was writing with a limited understanding of what he was seeing, so he used similes to describe what he could not fully grasp. When he said that "something like a great mountain burning with fire was thrown into the sea," he was likely describing an asteroid.

The journal *Science* claimed that there is a 1 in 300 chance the near-Earth asteroid 1950 DA will hit Earth on March 16, 2880. It is one kilometer wide—that is a little more than half a mile. And researchers say the impact of a half-mile wide asteroid would be the equivalent of 100,000 megatons of TNT.[1]

This asteroid would have a significant impact on marine life. And consider the stench of death. People say, "Protect the rainforest," but the rainforest is not what provides the most oxygen for our planet. Plankton does. Scientists estimate plankton provides 50 to 80 percent of Earth's oxygen.[2] Along with the destruction of the "green grass," people will be gasping for air, and the air will smell like decay.

Also consider that at any one time, there are about 50,000 merchant ships on the sea carrying five to six million containers of goods.[3] Imagine what the destruction of one-third of the commercial ships worldwide will do to economies globally and to the availability of goods.

Third Trumpet

> **REVELATION 8:10-11**—"The third angel sounded: And a great star fell from heaven, burning like a torch, and it fell on a third of the rivers and on the springs of water. The name of the star is Wormwood. A third of the waters became wormwood, and many men died from the water, because it was made bitter."

The "great star burning like a torch" could be another asteroid or comet. This "star" is called "Wormwood," which is literally a plant used for medicinal purposes and figuratively a sign of God's judgment. While trumpet number two's judgment will fall on the oceans, trumpet number three's judgment will fall on rivers and springs, turning a third of the world's fresh water bitter. Perhaps something in the bitterness of the water is poisonous, or people die of thirst. But because the drinking water is compromised, many die.

This resembles a catastrophe that happened on April 26, 1986, in Chernobyl, Ukraine. There, a nuclear plant had a partial meltdown, causing eight tons of radioactive material to escape into the atmosphere. There were 8,000 sudden deaths, and another 200,000 people suffering the effects of the accident. Scientists say that because of the radiation that leaked into the atmosphere, it will be another 20,000 years before Chernobyl will be inhabitable again.[4] People lost their lives, possessions, and homes.

On July 26, 1986, *The New York Times* featured an article about a Russian writer who pointed out that the Ukrainian word translated "wormwood" was Chernobyl.[5] For this reason, some consider this meltdown a fulfillment of the prophecy of the third trumpet. But the events of Chernobyl from 1986 would be better understood as a tragic glimpse into the future devastation that will come upon Earth when the third trumpet is blown.

Fourth Trumpet

> **REVELATION 8:12**—"The fourth angel sounded: And a third of the sun was struck, a third of the moon, and a third of the stars, so that a third of them were darkened. A third of the day did not shine, and likewise the night."

All the light sources are darkened by a third, disrupting the day-night cycle, as Jesus predicted:

> **Luke 21:25a**—"There will be signs in the sun, in the moon, and in the stars; and on the earth distress of nations, with perplexity, the sea and the waves roaring."

And because the world will be darker, Earth will be colder.

Eagle or Angel

> **REVELATION 8:13a**—"I looked, and I heard an angel flying through the midst of heaven..."

Some translations say "eagle" instead of "angel" because the Greek word is not *angelos*, meaning "angel," but *aetós*, meaning "eagle." But this is not a contradiction. This is likely an angel that has features like those of an eagle. Remember how Revelation 4 describes one of the angelic living creatures as having a face like an eagle.

Revelation 4:7—"The first living creature was like a lion, the second living creature like a calf, the third living creature had a face like a man, and the fourth living creature was like a flying eagle."

Warning

> **REVELATION 8:13b**–"...saying with a loud voice, 'Woe, woe, woe to the inhabitants of the earth, because of the remaining blasts of the trumpet of the three angels who are about to sound!'"

The worst is yet to come.

Reflections on Revelation 8

Getting Started

Revelation 8 begins and ends with foreboding—first, a silence in heaven (Revelation 8:1b), and then a warning that God would increase the intensity of the tribulation (Revelation 8:13b). How does this point to the fervor we should have in reaching the lost (see Romans 10:14-15; Ephesians 5:15-16)?

Study Questions

1. What is the significance of God saving specific angels for the purpose of heralding God's trumpet judgments in Revelation 8:2? How does this principle apply to our lives (see Esther 4:14; 1 Corinthians 7:12-24)?
2. What does the description of God's temple in chapter 8 reveal about the plans God gave to Moses and David (see Hebrews 8:5)? How should we continue to live after the pattern of God's kingdom (Matthew 6:10; Romans 12:2)?
3. What happens as the prayers of the saints go up (Revelation 8:3-5)? How should that impact how we treat prayer?
4. In the first trumpet judgment, what does the phrase "mingled with blood" (Revelation 8:7) probably refer to? Compare this judgment with what happens to the saints in Revelation 7:13-14—what are the two options all men have (see 1 John 5:12)?
5. How do the trumpet judgments strike at the idolatrous worship of creation (see Romans 1:25)? And why is this judgment relevant to our culture?
6. Besides creation, what idol do the trumpet judgments strike against according to Revelation 8:9b (see Luke 12:15; 1 Timothy 6:10)?

7. In the Bible, what does wormwood symbolize (Revelation 8:10-11)? What wickedness amid Earth's population is God trying to point to when He uses this symbol (see Proverbs 5:3-4; Jeremiah 9:13-15, 23:15; Amos 5:7; 6:12)?
8. John was limited in his contextual understanding of what God revealed to him, so he used various ways to describe asteroids and comets (Revelation 8:10). How does this inform our reading of Revelation?
9. How can Chernobyl serve as a glimpse of the third trumpet judgment of Revelation 8:10? Why do you think God gave us this glimpse (see Ezekiel 18:32)?
10. The fourth trumpet judgment drags the world into darkness; what is the symbolism of this judgment (see John 3:19; 12:46; Colossians 1:13; 1 Thessalonians 5:5)? By contrast, how are believers called to walk?

Important Takeaways for Us Today

1. The fourth trumpet judgment attacks the idol of astrology (Luke 21:25; Revelation 8:12). Why is astrology anti-God (see Deuteronomy 4:19; 2 Kings 17:16; Daniel 2:27-28), and why do some believers still tolerate or even believe in astrology (see Acts 17:11; Ephesians 4:11-14)?
2. Revelation 8 shows God both judging mankind and striking against the idols they have chosen over Him, such as nature, material possessions, and the stars of heaven. If God spoke to your heart, what idols would He call attention to? What does God want instead?

9

Out of the Abyss

REVELATION 9

When we kick God out of our world, we inevitably welcome demons in. This will culminate in the events of Revelation 9, where we see that the demons of the abyss and those chained under the Euphrates River are unleashed. These are the worst of the worst demons, deemed too evil to be allowed to roam freely. But these severe trials are not purposeless—they are to warn unbelievers that these are the demons they are choosing to dorm with for eternity if they do not repent. As we read Revelation 9, remember that in these tribulations, God is seeking to bring men back to Himself.

Background

Satan's Names

In Revelation 9, terms like "star," "locusts," "scorpions," "Abaddon," "Apollyon," "angels who are bound," and "army" all describe Satan or his demonic forces.

Demonic Appearances

Demons will appear during trumpet number five, when God allows them to torment people but not to kill them. With trumpet number six, God will allow demons to kill a third of Earth's population—an estimated nearly 2 billion people.

Fifth Trumpet

Fallen Star

> **REVELATION 9:1-2a**—"The fifth angel sounded: And I saw a star fallen from heaven to the earth. To him was given the key to the bottomless pit. And he opened the bottomless pit."

Previously in Revelation, "star" described something like an asteroid or a comet, but this time, John gave the star masculine pronouns, informing us this is not a cosmological star, but a being.

We use the same slang in our language, too, when we call a famous person a star.

This is also not the only time the Bible refers to an angel as a "star":

> **Revelation 1:20**—"The mystery of the seven stars which you saw in My right hand, and the seven golden lampstands: The seven stars are the angels of the seven churches, and the seven lampstands which you saw are the seven churches."

And the Bible has described Satan in a similar manner before:

> **Luke 10:18**—"He said to them, 'I saw Satan fall like lightning from heaven.'"

> **Isaiah 14:12 (ESV)**—"How you are fallen from heaven, O Day Star, son of Dawn! How you are cut down to the ground, you who laid the nations low!" The KJV and NKJV translations say "Lucifer" instead of "Day Star," but other translations say "morning star." Also, "Lucifer" comes from the Latin root words *lux* and *ferre*, meaning "light carrier."

Ezekiel 28:16b-17a—"Therefore I cast you as a profane thing out of the mountain of God; and I destroyed you, O covering cherub, from the midst of the fiery stones. Your heart was lifted up because of your beauty; you corrupted your wisdom for the sake of your splendor; I cast you to the ground."

Bottomless Pit

REVELATION 9:1b-2—"To him was given the key to the bottomless pit. And he opened the bottomless pit, and smoke arose out of the pit like the smoke of a great furnace. So the sun and the air were darkened because of the smoke of the pit."

The bottomless pit is called the "abyss" in some translations, taken from the Greek word *abussos*. It is used seven times in Revelation, and two other times elsewhere.

Luke 8:30-31—"Jesus asked him, saying, 'What is your name?' And he said, 'Legion,' because many demons had entered him. And they begged Him that He would not command them to go out into the abyss."

These demons are afraid of going to the abyss, for the abyss is a cavernous hole in the earth where the worst demons are sent.

2 Peter 2:4—"God did not spare the angels who sinned, but cast them down to hell and delivered them into chains of darkness, to be reserved for judgment."

Jude 1:6—"The angels who did not keep their proper domain, but left their own abode, He has reserved in everlasting chains under darkness for the judgment of the great day."

But here in Revelation, the pit opens, and the worst of the demons are unleashed.

Location

We do not know where the bottomless pit is, only that its demons were released for this purpose: judgment. But we can speculate. Seismologists determined the core of the earth is roughly twice the size of the moon, solid, mostly iron, and the hottest part is 10,800 degrees Fahrenheit, as hot as the surface of the sun.[1]

We speculate the abyss is somewhere in the center of the earth. In fact, David references this in Psalm 63:9: "Those who seek my life, to destroy it, shall go into the lower parts of the earth."

Locusts

> **REVELATION 9:3-4**—"Out of the smoke locusts came upon the earth. And to them was given power, as the scorpions of the earth have power. They were commanded not to harm the grass of the earth, or any green thing, or any tree, but only those men who do not have the seal of God on their foreheads."

These are not literal locusts. They do not harm any plant or tree, which is what locusts typically do. Instead, they torment those without God's seal on their foreheads.

And they do this for five months.

> **REVELATION 9:5**—"They were not given authority to kill them, but to torment them for five months. Their torment was like the torment of a scorpion when it strikes a man."

God is trying to get the attention of unbelievers, but He has parameters: five months and no deaths. And though the unsaved will be so tormented as to want to take their own lives, God, as the author of life, will not let them:

REVELATION 9:6—"In those days men will seek death and will not find it; they will desire to die, and death will flee from them."

These demons also look nothing like locusts, but rather, a conglomeration of animals with men's faces.

REVELATION 9:7-9—"The shape of the locusts was like horses prepared for battle. On their heads were crowns of something like gold, and their faces were like the faces of men. They had hair like women's hair, and their teeth were like lions' teeth. And they had breastplates like breastplates of iron, and the sound of their wings was like the sound of chariots with many horses running into battle."

Some interpret these creatures to be helicopters, especially because the "wings" make such a loud noise, like the noise of a helicopter, and they have men's faces, like windows showing pilots' faces. However, this should be interpreted more literally—demons that come out of the abyss.

Abaddon/Apollyon

These locusts have a king over them, and his name is Abaddon.

REVELATION 9:10-11—"They had tails like scorpions, and there were stings in their tails. Their power was to hurt men five months. And they had as king over them the angel of the bottomless pit, whose name in Hebrew is Abaddon, but in Greek he has the name Apollyon."

Again, these are not real locusts, because, as Solomon stated:

Proverbs 30:27—"The locusts have no king, yet they all advance in ranks."

But these demonic locusts do have a king. *Abaddon* in the Hebrew, or *Apollyon* in Greek, mean the same thing: "Destroyer." This is a reference to Satan, king of the demonic legion, sitting at the top of hell's rankings.

> **Ephesians 6:12**—"We do not wrestle against flesh and blood, but against principalities, against powers, against the rulers of the darkness of this age, against spiritual hosts of wickedness in the heavenly places."

Similarly, there are rankings in heaven: Michael is listed as an archangel, Gabriel as a messenger angel, and Lucifer—before he rebelled—was a guardian cherub (Ezekiel 28:14).

Sixth Trumpet

Demons of Euphrates

The demons released at the fifth trumpet will come out of the bottomless pit, but the demons released at the sixth trumpet will come out of the depths of the Euphrates River.

> **REVELATION 9:12-14**–"One woe is past. Behold, still two more woes are coming after these things. Then the sixth angel sounded: And I heard a voice from the four horns of the golden altar which is before God, saying to the sixth angel who had the trumpet, 'Release the four angels who are bound at the great river Euphrates.'"

We know these are fallen angels because they are "bound." And unlike the demons of the abyss, these are allowed to kill.

Euphrates River

The Euphrates River was one of four rivers in the Garden of Eden (Genesis 2:14). This reference to the Euphrates River places the location of these demons in ancient Babylon, which is modern-day Iraq. The Bible references this later in Revelation 18.

> **Revelation 18:2**—"He cried mightily with a loud voice, saying, 'Babylon the great is fallen, is fallen, and has become a dwelling place of demons, a prison for every foul spirit, and a cage for every unclean and hated bird!'"

When you look at the ancient story of Babel in the book of Genesis, "Babel" is Babylon, and there, men worshipped the stars and the heavenly hosts. All occult worship began in ancient Babylon, and the effect and presence of the occult is still there and will return in force during the tribulation.

The Hour and Day

> **REVELATION 9:15a**–"The four angels, who had been prepared for the hour and day and month and year…"

This shows that God is specific and intentional with these trials.

One-Third Killed

> **REVELATION 9:15b**–The four angels "were released to kill a third of mankind."

A third of Earth's remaining population—an estimated 1.5 billion people (after a continual decline with the various judgments up to this point)—will die.

Army of Horsemen

> **REVELATION 9:16**–"Now the number of the army of the horsemen was two hundred million; I heard the number of them."

In 1965, *Time* magazine featured an article in which China boasted that it could put forth an army of 200 million men. Some Christians took this as a fulfillment of biblical prophecy about the army, but China could be embellishing this number.

Consider that the total combined number of soldiers involved in World War II was 70 million, so 200 million is an astronomically high number.

This could be an army of men led by demons, men possessed by demons, or a literal demon army. But the context suggests an army related to demonic principalities.

> **REVELATION 9:17**—"I saw the horses in the vision: those who sat on them had breastplates of fiery red, hyacinth blue, and sulfur yellow; and the heads of the horses were like the heads of lions; and out of their mouths came fire, smoke, and brimstone."

The "fire, smoke, and brimstone" is what will kill people.

> **REVELATION 9:18-19**—"By these three plagues a third of mankind was killed—by the fire and the smoke and the brimstone which came out of their mouths. For their power is in their mouth and in their tails; for their tails are like serpents, having heads; and with them they do harm."

Again, this army is unlikely to be human. Their mouths and tails do not sound human. The fire and brimstone coming out of their mouths gives them away.

Unrepentant

> **REVELATION 9:20**—"But the rest of mankind, who were not killed by these plagues, did not repent of the works of their hands, that they should not worship demons, and idols of gold, silver, brass, stone, and wood, which can neither see nor hear nor walk."

Despite these judgments, people did not repent. What will it take to convince them?

God's heart is for people to repent, and that is why "repent" is found 12 times in the book of Revelation—more times than in any other New Testament book.

"Repent" is *metanoeō* in the Greek text, stemming from two words: *meta*, meaning "to change," and *noeō*, meaning "your mind or your will." Hence, repentance is the exercise of your mind and will to change the path you are on, turning from sin to Christ.

> **REVELATION 9:21**—"They did not repent of their murders or their sorceries or their sexual immorality or their thefts."

Many will choose to cling to their "sorceries." In your Bible, you might have a footnote on the word "sorceries," mentioning it can be interpreted as "drugs." This is because the Greek word here is *pharmakeia*, which is where we get our English word *pharmacy*. So, the Bible is not talking about sorcery here, but drugs. The people who remain want to keep their sin more than their lives. Despite seeing God judge the wicked, they hold tight to their wickedness.

Consider that by now, Earth's population is significantly lower. Christians have been raptured, one-fourth of the population (roughly 2 billion people) will die at the fourth seal judgment, and many tribulation Christians will have been martyred. The global population could be down to less than 4 billion! By the time you get to the sixth trumpet judgment, half of Earth's population is gone.

At a minimum, 4 billion people are gone by the midway point of the tribulation. But they remain stubborn, so God will turn up the heat.

Reflections on Revelation 9

Getting Started

In Revelation 9, despite the demonic forces at work, we see that God is in control even over them, specifying when they are unleashed, for how long, and what they are allowed to do (Revelation 9:2, 4-5, 15). How does the lordship and sovereignty of our God affect your view of world events?

Study Questions

1. Satan is called "a star fallen from heaven" (Revelation 9:1). What does this name allude to about his history (see Isaiah 14:12; Ezekiel 28:16-17; Luke 10:18) and the danger of pride (see Psalm 138:6; Proverbs 16:18; 1 Corinthians 10:12; James 4:6)?
2. Revelation 9:1-2 mentions demons from the abyss. What is significant about them in comparison to other demons (see Luke 8:30-31; 2 Peter 2:4; and Jude 1:6)?
3. Who is Abaddon (Revelation 9:10-11), and what does his role tell us about how hell's forces function (see Ephesians 6:12)?
4. The demons that come unbound at the sixth trumpet judgment rise from the Euphrates River (Revelation 9:12-14), which was in ancient Babylon, or in modern-day Iraq. Why is this location significant?
5. What does the exact length and extent of the locusts' torment of men and the phrase "prepared for the hour and day and month and year" (Revelation 9:3-5, 15) tell us about God's character?
6. Some believe the army of horsemen (Revelation 9:16) will be an army of men led or possessed by demons, but what makes

this theory unlikely (Revelation 9:17-19)? What is the danger of not reading the Bible in its proper context (2 Peter 3:16)?

7. How did unbelievers react to the fifth and sixth trumpet judgments (Revelation 9:6, 20-21)? What are some reasons you see people cling to worldly solutions to problems like drugs rather than coming to God for living water (see Jeremiah 2:13)?
8. What does the word "repent" mean (see Revelation 9:20)? As believers, we still repent, though not to attain salvation (see John 13:10). How do you tend to repent? As soon as you sin (1 John 1:7)? Or do you feel distant from God for a time before you eventually come to Him for forgiveness (see Hebrews 4:16)?
9. What does the Greek word that Revelation 9:21 translated as "sorceries" mean? How does this affect the reading of this verse?

Important Takeaways for Us Today

1. What leads to the sin of pride that made the enemy fall (see Psalm 10:4), and how do we avoid pride (see Ecclesiastes 5:2; Romans 12:3, 16; 1 Corinthians 4:7)?
2. How are we able to defeat the organization and rankings of hell's forces described in Revelation 9:10-11 (see Ephesians 6:11-18; 1 Peter 5:8-9)?

10

A Bittersweet Prophecy

REVELATION 10

Imagine a mighty angel—whose head reaches the clouds and whose feet touch the land and sea—coming up to you and telling you to "eat this book." Would you eat it? Sounds strange, doesn't it? Yet that's what John was told to do. He was given a small book, symbolizing the words of this prophecy, and told by a mighty angel to eat it. Let us examine its bittersweet contents.

Background

An Interlude

Here, we arrive at the longest interlude between judgments. Usually, seal judgments are opened one after another, trumpet judgments sounded one after another, and bowl judgments poured one after another. But between the sixth and seventh trumpet, there's an interlude.

This is likely because of God's mercy. He will give men a chance to repent before He brings more judgment. And we know from the end of Revelation 9 that, sadly, men will not repent.

A Mighty Angel and a Book

A Lengthy Vision

> **REVELATION 10:1a**–"I saw still another mighty angel coming."

John started chapter 10 with the words, "I saw." This is his longest-recorded vision because we do not see the words "I saw" again until Revelation 13:1.

Another Mighty Angel

> **REVELATION 10:1**–"I saw still another mighty angel coming down from heaven, clothed with a cloud. And a rainbow was on his head, his face was like the sun, and his feet like pillars of fire."

We have already seen mighty angels, hence the words "still another." But who is he? Some Bible scholars believe this is Jesus for these reasons:

1. He is clothed with a cloud

   Revelation 1:7a—"Behold, He is coming with clouds."

2. He has a rainbow around his head

   Revelation 4:3—"He who sat there was like a jasper and a sardius stone in appearance; and there was a rainbow around the throne, in appearance like an emerald."

3. He has a countenance like the sun

   Revelation 1:16—"He had in His right hand seven stars, out of His mouth went a sharp two-edged sword, and His countenance was like the sun shining in its strength."

4. He has feet like pillars of fire

   Revelation 1:15—"His feet were like fine brass, as if refined in a furnace, and His voice as the sound of many waters."

Other Bible scholars disagree, and so do I. Jesus is never described as an angel in the book of Revelation.

Now, sometimes in the Old Testament, Jesus is called the Angel of the Lord. However, these Christophanies, or appearances of Christ, all happen prior to the virgin birth.

Another

Also, the word for "another" is the Greek term *allon*, meaning "another of the same kind," and if John wanted to distinguish this mighty angel from those who came before, he could have used the word *heteros*, "another of a different kind."

Also, this mighty angel comes to Earth between the sixth and seventh trumpet judgments, but Jesus does not come to Earth again until the end of the tribulation (Revelation 19).

So, who is the mighty angel? It is only a matter of speculation, but this is probably Michael the archangel (Jude 1:9), the only archangel listed in the Bible.

If this is Michael, it would explain the similarities between him and Jesus, for his name—*Mikha'el* in Hebrew—literally means "who is like God?" And because he is meant to represent the presence, authority, and power of the Lord, it makes sense that he would reflect some of Jesus' qualities.

Land and Sea

> **REVELATION 10:2**–"He had a little book open in his hand. And he set his right foot on the sea and his left foot on the land."

This symbolizes that this angel is given authority over the land and sea.

Seven Thunders

> **REVELATION 10:3–**"[He] cried with a loud voice, as when a lion roars. When he cried out, seven thunders uttered their voices."

These "seven thunders" may refer to the voice of God, because when David wrote about God's voice, he described it seven separate times.

> **Psalm 29:3-9**—"The voice of the LORD is over the waters; the God of glory thunders; the LORD is over many waters. The voice of the LORD is powerful; the voice of the LORD is full of majesty.
>
> "The voice of the LORD breaks the cedars, yes, the LORD splinters the cedars of Lebanon. He makes them also skip like a calf, Lebanon and Sirion like a young wild ox. The voice of the LORD divides the flames of fire.
>
> "The voice of the LORD shakes the wilderness; the LORD shakes the Wilderness of Kadesh. The voice of the LORD makes the deer give birth, and strips the forests bare; and in His temple everyone says, 'Glory!'"

Hence, these "seven thunders" are probably aspects of God's divine wrath, which God ordered John not to write about:

> **REVELATION 10:4–**"Now when the seven thunders uttered their voices, I was about to write; but I heard a voice from heaven saying to me, 'Seal up the things which the seven thunders uttered, and do not write them.'"

The Oath

> **REVELATION 10:5-6–**"The angel whom I saw standing on the sea and on the land raised up his hand to heaven and swore by

> Him who lives forever and ever, who created heaven and the things that are in it, the earth and the things that are in it, and the sea and the things that are in it, that there should be delay no longer."

In other words, there comes a point when there is no turning back.

> **REVELATION 10:7**–"In the days of the sounding of the seventh angel, when he is about to sound, the mystery of God would be finished, as He declared to His servants the prophets."

God's plan for the ages is about to unfold here. The things He prophesied by the prophets will come to pass.

John Eats the Book

> **REVELATION 10:8**–"The voice which I heard from heaven spoke to me again and said, 'Go, take the little book which is open in the hand of the angel who stands on the sea and on the earth.'"

Luckily, this is a short book, just as the tribulation is a relatively short but heavy time of judgment.

> **REVELATION 10:9**–"I went to the angel and said to him, 'Give me the little book.' And he said to me, 'Take and eat it; and it will make your stomach bitter, but it will be as sweet as honey in your mouth.'"

This book is bittersweet: Bitter because the judgments are harsh, but sweet because God still allows people the opportunity to repent.

The Nourishing Word

> **REVELATION 10:10**–"I took the little book out of the angel's hand and ate it, and it was as sweet as honey in my mouth. But when I had eaten it, my stomach became bitter."

This is symbolic of being sustained by God's Word, of getting Scripture into your soul:

> **Ezekiel 3:1-4**—"He said to me, 'Son of man, eat what you find; eat this scroll, and go, speak to the house of Israel.' So I opened my mouth, and He caused me to eat that scroll.
>
> "And He said to me, 'Son of man, feed your belly, and fill your stomach with this scroll that I give you.' So I ate, and it was in my mouth like honey in sweetness.
>
> "Then He said to me: 'Son of man, go to the house of Israel and speak with My words to them.'"
>
> **Psalm 119:103**—"How sweet are Your words to my taste, sweeter than honey to my mouth!"

Prophesy

> **REVELATION 10:11**–"He said to me, 'You must prophesy again about many peoples, nations, tongues, and kings.'"

Just as the word went into John, he was now responsible to deliver it to the nations. We cannot keep God's Word to ourselves.

Reflections on Revelation 10

Getting Started

Between the sixth and seventh trumpet judgments lies Revelation 10, a chapter where an angel who prepares to carry out God's wrath first hands John a book (Revelation 10:9-10). How does this bittersweet book give us insight into God's reason for this time of tribulation (see Romans 10:14-15) and into the warning embedded in Revelation (see Psalm 119:103; John 6:60; 2 Corinthians 2:14-16)?

Study Questions

1. After the previous judgments halved the world's population, John recorded the longest interlude between judgments, beginning in chapter 10. What does the interlude tell us about God?
2. Who do some speculate is the mighty angel of Revelation 10:1 (see Jude 1:9)? How does the angel's glory point back to God (see Revelation 4:11)?
3. When John described the mighty angel in Revelation 10:1, he said the angel was clothed with a cloud, had a rainbow about his head, appeared like the sun, and had feet like pillars of fire—all characteristics that he shares with Jesus (see Revelation 1:7; 4:3; 1:16; 1:15). How do these similarities show God's attributes (see Exodus 16:10; 19:9; Genesis 9:13; Malachi 4:2; Luke 1:78-79; Nehemiah 9:12; Revelation 1:15-16)?
4. Why is the mighty angel atop the land and sea in Revelation 10:2? Why do you think God sometimes gives power to His servants rather than executing His will Himself (see 1 Corinthians 1:26-29; 2 Corinthians 12:9)?

5. What are the seven thunders of Revelation 10:3 (see Psalm 29:3-9)? Why do we as believers not have to worry about being under God's wrath anymore (see John 3:36)?
6. The angel's oath confirms that God will do as He promised (Revelation 10:5-6). How have you witnessed the faithfulness of God?
7. Why did John eat the book, and why is the book sweet and bitter (see Ezekiel 3:1-4; Matthew 4:4; 24:22; Revelation 10:8-10)? How are we called to treat God's book, the Bible (see Deuteronomy 11:18; Psalm 119:9-11; 2 Timothy 3:16-17)?
8. Just as Jesus delivered His Word to John for him to deliver to the nations (Revelation 10:11), so He has given His Word to us to share with others. Who has God called you to witness to, and how will you share the gospel with them this week?

Important Takeaways for Us Today

1. We do not have the ability to mimic God's power like the mighty angel of Revelation 10:1, but we can mimic His character (see 2 Corinthians 3:18; 1 Peter 2:21). In what ways do you feel convicted to resemble Christ more (see John 15:12-13; Romans 6:1-14; 1 Corinthians 13:4-8; 1 Peter 2:19-23)?
2. Describe how each of the seven voices of God (Psalm 29:3-9) affect your understanding of God's sovereign dominion over Earth:

    a. The voice of the Lord is over the waters.

    b. The voice of the Lord is powerful.

    c. The voice of the Lord is full of majesty.

    d. The voice of the Lord breaks the cedars.

e. The voice of the Lord divides the flames of fire.

f. The voice of the Lord shakes the wilderness.

g. The voice of the Lord makes deer give birth and strips the forests bare.

11

A Call to Repentance

REVELATION 11

Revelation 11 is a wild ride. We read about men blowing fire out of their mouths, water turned to blood, murder plots, and resurrections. But do not let all that distract you from the central theme of this chapter: Jesus' ever-persistent love for the lost, giving them time and time again a chance to repent.

The Two Witnesses

Temple of God

> **REVELATION 11:1**–"I was given a reed like a measuring rod. And the angel stood, saying, 'Rise and measure the temple of God, the altar, and those who worship there.'"

Remember, Roman Emperor Titus Vespasian brought down the temple when he conquered Jerusalem in AD 70. When John wrote this in the 90s AD, the temple had been destroyed for at least 20 years.

We see here a prophecy that the temple will be rebuilt after the

Antichrist establishes a seven-year peace agreement between Israel and the rest of the Middle East (Daniel 9:27). In the middle of the seven-year agreement, the Antichrist will declare himself to be God (2 Thessalonians 2:4), and the Jews will realize they were duped, and that the Antichrist is not their Messiah.

Currently, there is no temple on the Temple Mount. Instead, there are the Dome of the Rock and the Al-Aqsa Mosque, along with other Muslim structures.

In past years, on Tisha B'av (the ninth of Av), zealous Jews have marched to the Temple Mount in an effort to lay the cornerstone for a new temple, but this act is only symbolic because the Jews know the Muslims will turn them away.

The Jews do not have possession of the Temple Mount. This is because after Israel's victory in the 1967 Six-Day War, Minister of Defense Moshe Dayan made an agreement with Muslim authorities that they could maintain administrative rights to the Temple Mount. Israelis later regretted this decision, and for this reason, there is no statue or portrait of Moshe Dayan in Israel. Though Muslims currently refuse to allow the Jews to build their temple on the mount, there will come a day when the Antichrist persuades Muslims to allow it.

Gentiles at the Temple

> **REVELATION 11:2-3**—"Leave out the court which is outside the temple, and do not measure it, for it has been given to the Gentiles. And they will tread the holy city underfoot for forty-two months. And I will give power to my two witnesses, and they will prophesy one thousand two hundred and sixty days, clothed in sackcloth."

Forty-two months is 3.5 years, and 1,260 days is also 3.5 years if you use the Babylonian calendar, which had 360 days per year. But the Bible uses both forms to indicate the separate halves of the tribulation: By using "months" in verse 2 and "days" in verse 3, God distinguishes the first and second halves of the tribulation. The first half is described in days, and the latter half in months.

And during that latter half, the Gentiles will tread upon the Temple Mount because the Antichrist will proclaim himself to be God at the halfway point of the tribulation, allowing for the heathen takeover of the temple.

Sackcloth

> **REVELATION 11:3–**"I will give power to my two witnesses, and they will prophesy one thousand two hundred and sixty days, clothed in sackcloth."

The two witnesses dress in "sackcloth," as is customary of prophets who grieve for their people, and they are commissioned to proclaim the gospel to the nations. These two witnesses minister during the first half of the tribulation.

They also look out of place because they are from the past and dressed as such.

Fire from Their Mouths

> **REVELATION 11:4-5–**"These are the two olive trees and the two lampstands standing before the God of the earth. And if anyone wants to harm them, fire proceeds from their mouth and devours their enemies. And if anyone wants to harm them, he must be killed in this manner."

To protect the two witnesses, God gives them the ability to produce fire from their mouths.

Who They Are

Who are these two witnesses? Some believe they are Joshua the high priest and Zerubbabel the governor, because in Zechariah 4, these men are described as "olive trees" and "lampstands."

Another school of thought says these two witnesses are Elijah and Enoch because both men were taken up to be with the Lord and never experienced death.

Yet the majority view is that the witnesses will be Elijah and Moses, the same men who appeared with Jesus on the Mount of Transfiguration in Matthew 17.

> **Malachi 4:4-6**—"Remember the Law of Moses, my servant, which I commanded him in Horeb for all Israel, with the statutes and judgments. Behold, I will send you Elijah the prophet before the coming of the great and dreadful day of the LORD. And he will turn the hearts of the fathers to the children, and the hearts of the children to their fathers, lest I come and strike the earth with a curse."

This leads us to believe that the representatives of the law and the prophets—Moses and Elijah—will come to warn the world before the end.

When Jesus brought Peter, James, and John to the Mount of Transfiguration, they saw Moses and Elijah, signifying to us their importance and how God was not done with their story.

> **Matthew 17:3**—"Behold, Moses and Elijah appeared to them, talking with Him."

As an aside, Peter instinctively recognized Moses and Elijah, although they had died centuries before, which is a reminder to us that we will recognize and know our friends, loved ones, and even those whom we have never met!

The Powers of Moses and Elijah

We also know that the two witnesses have powers from God that we have seen before, specifically powers that Moses and Elijah used:

1. The power to shut heaven

> **REVELATION 11:6a**–"These have power to shut heaven, so that no rain falls in the days of their prophecy."

> **1 Kings 17:1**—"Elijah the Tishbite, of the inhabitants of Gilead, said to Ahab, 'As the LORD God of Israel lives, before whom I stand, there shall not be dew nor rain these years, except at my word.'" This drought persisted for 3.5 years, ending only when Elijah prayed for rain after the people repented at Mount Carmel.

> **James 5:17-18**—"Elijah was a man with a nature like ours, and he prayed earnestly that it would not rain; and it did not rain on the land for three years and six months. And he prayed again, and the heaven gave rain, and the earth produced its fruit."

2. The power to turn water to blood

> **REVELATION 11:6b**–"They have power over waters to turn them to blood, and to strike the earth with all plagues, as often as they desire."

> **Exodus 7:17**—The first of the ten plagues God executed involved Moses turning water to blood: "Thus says the LORD: 'By this you shall know that I am the LORD. Behold, I will strike the waters which are in the river with the rod that is in my hand, and they shall be turned to blood.'"

The Witnesses Murdered

> **REVELATION 11:7**—"When they finish their testimony, the beast that ascends out of the bottomless pit will make war against them, overcome them, and kill them."

The Antichrist will kill the two witnesses. He is not stronger than God, but God will allow him to kill His two witnesses once they have said all that they needed to say.

> **REVELATION 11:8**—"Their dead bodies will lie in the street of the great city which spiritually is called Sodom and Egypt, where also our Lord was crucified."

The phrase "where also our Lord was crucified" gives us the location of these two witnesses: Jerusalem, which is known spiritually as "Sodom and Egypt" because it had fallen into sin.

> **REVELATION 11:9-10**—"Those from the peoples, tribes, tongues, and nations will see their dead bodies three-and-a-half days, and not allow their dead bodies to be put into graves. And those who dwell on the earth will rejoice over them, make merry, and send gifts to one another, because these two prophets tormented those who dwell on the earth."

Of course, sometimes the truth is tormenting, and so is the fire the two witnesses will breathe out against those who try to kill them. They will have tried to lead unbelievers to Jesus, the Savior who could save their souls. In return for their witness, unbelievers will celebrate their deaths as if it were a new holiday and will not even give them a respectable burial. But God will get the last word.

Just as all the people of the world will see their deaths, so they will see their resurrections.

The Witnesses Resurrected

> **REVELATION 11:11**—"Now after the three-and-a-half days the breath of life from God entered them, and they stood on their feet, and great fear fell on those who saw them."

You bet they will be afraid!

> **REVELATION 11:12**—"They heard a loud voice from heaven saying to them, 'Come up here.' And they ascended to heaven in a cloud, and their enemies saw them."

Praise God for this testimony! After the crucifixion, it looked like God lost, until Jesus got the last laugh and rose from the dead. The same will happen with the two witnesses. Things are not always as they first appear.

> **REVELATION 11:13**—"In the same hour there was a great earthquake, and a tenth of the city fell. In the earthquake seven thousand people were killed, and the rest were afraid and gave glory to the God of heaven."

As a result of these events, the fear of God will grip people's hearts and turn some of them to God.

The Seventh Trumpet

The Announcement

We have made it through six of the seven trumpets, and now, this intermission is done.

REVELATION 11:14—"The second woe is past. Behold, the third woe is coming quickly."

Then God has an angel blow the seventh trumpet and announce how Christ will soon take over the earth as Judge and King.

REVELATION 11:15—"Then the seventh angel sounded: And there were loud voices in heaven, saying, 'The kingdoms of this world have become the kingdoms of our Lord and of His Christ, and He shall reign forever and ever!'"

The 24 Elders

REVELATION 11:16-17—"And the twenty-four elders who sat before God on their thrones fell on their faces and worshiped God, saying: 'We give You thanks, O Lord God Almighty, the One who is and who was and who is to come, because You have taken Your great power and reigned.'"

Revelation mentions three times that the 24 elders, who represent the church, fall on their faces to worship God:

1. Revelation 4, when they praise God as Creator
2. Revelation 5, when they praise God as Redeemer
3. Revelation 11, when they praise God as Judge and King

In Heaven

> **REVELATION 11:18-19**—"'The nations were angry, and Your wrath has come, and the time of the dead, that they should be judged, and that You should reward Your servants the prophets and the saints, and those who fear Your name, small and great, and should destroy those who destroy the earth.'
>
> "Then the temple of God was opened in heaven, and the ark of His covenant was seen in His temple. And there were lightnings, noises, thunderings, an earthquake, and great hail."

This scene happens in heaven, and these "thunderings" signify the power and presence of God.

Reflections on Revelation 11

Getting Started

In Revelation 11:15, amid accounts of God's judgments on unrepentant mankind, heaven declares Jesus' coming victory. How should we view events in Revelation and in our lives, knowing that Christ will have the final say?

Study Questions

1. Why did John record the measurements of the temple of God (Revelation 11:1) when the temple had already been torn down for at least 20 years in his time?
2. What will set the Jewish people up to be so deceived by the Antichrist? What sets people up even now to be deceived by the enemy (see 2 Thessalonians 2:8-12)?
3. In Revelation 11:2-3, how did John distinguish between the first and second halves of the tribulation, and why do the Gentiles tread upon the temple area during the second half?
4. What role does God give the two witnesses (Revelation 11:3)? What does this say about how God views the importance of reaching the lost (see Matthew 18:12-14)?
5. Revelation 11:3 shows the two witnesses in sackcloth, the customary grieving apparel of prophets. Why are these two witnesses grieving (see Romans 9:1-5)? Is there anyone you have a burden for, and in what ways can you pray for opportunities to witness to him/her?
6. Who are the two witnesses (see Revelation 11:3-5; Malachi 4:4-6; Matthew 17:3) and what do they represent (see Leviticus 18:5; Malachi 4:5; Matthew 22:37-40; Luke 16:29-31)? How should Christians view the Old Testament—the

law and the prophets—in light of the two witnesses' return (see Matthew 5:17-18; Hebrews 10:1-2, 9-12)?

7. What does the timing of the witnesses' deaths in Revelation 11:7-11 tell you about how God works amid tragedies (see Genesis 50:20; Romans 8:28; Romans 9:17)?
8. How does the testimony of the two witnesses (Revelation 11:7-13) parallel the lesson of Jesus' death and resurrection (see Acts 2:22-24)? How can you take comfort from these two accounts regarding this life and the life to come (see John 11:25-26; Romans 8:11, 35-39)?
9. In Revelation 11:15, the angel announces Jesus' coming victory as Judge and King. How should these two titles for Him influence how we live (see Matthew 28:18-20; 1 Timothy 6:6, 9-15; Hebrews 10:28-30; James 5:9)?
10. What are the two responses people will have to God's judgments (Revelation 11:13, 18)? What does this teach us about man's free will (see Matthew 28:17; John 6:64; Acts 28:23-24)?

Important Takeaways for Us Today

1. In Revelation, the 24 elders fall on their faces in worship three times. Describe how God has shown up in these various ways in your life and praise Him accordingly.
   a. In Revelation 4, God is praised as Creator
   b. In Revelation 5, God is praised as Redeemer
   c. In Revelation 11, God is praised as Judge and King

2. Though the two witnesses will have tried to lead people to the saving knowledge of Jesus, the people will celebrate their murder and dishonor their bodies (Revelation 11:7-11). What does Jesus want us to do in response to persecution (see Romans 12:14, 17-21; Matthew 5:10-12)?

12

A Temporary Reign of Terror

REVELATION 12

Imagine John, seeing a woman with a sun for her covering, a moon beneath her feet, and stars around her head. Would she not seem untouchable? Yet she is, for she runs from the dragon, hiding her child. Who is this woman, both strong and weak? Who is this dragon? This child? To understand chapter 12, we must understand that this chapter documents a symbolic representation of the history of the world. With that, let us dive in, remembering that Satan's reign is short.

The Woman, the Child, and the Dragon

Revelation 12 is a backdrop to end-times events, but also refers back to Genesis.

The Woman

Roman Catholics like to portray the Virgin Mary as the woman, their artists depicting her standing on a crescent moon with 12 stars around her head. Yet, the woman is called "a great sign," so this is not a literal woman.

Protestants believe this woman is the church, but the Bible refers to the church in female terms only when it calls her the bride of Christ. The Bible never calls her a woman giving birth. In fact, God birthed the church, not the other way around.

Mary Baker Eddy, the founder of Christian Science, claimed that she was the woman Revelation 12 spoke of and that the child the woman gave birth to is her religious system of Christian Science.

But the Bible is the best commentary on the Bible:

> **REVELATION 12:1**–"Now a great sign appeared in heaven: a woman clothed with the sun, with the moon under her feet, and on her head a garland of twelve stars."

> **Genesis 37:9**—"He [Joseph] dreamed still another dream and told it to his brothers, and said, 'Look, I have dreamed another dream. And this time, the sun, the moon, and the eleven stars bowed down to me.'"

The woman in Joseph's dream is described the same way as the woman in Revelation 12, meaning that the woman represents the nation of Israel.

And in Scripture, God consistently described Israel as a woman.

Isaiah 54—Israel is referred to as a barren woman.

Jeremiah 3—Israel is referred to as an adulterous woman.

Ezekiel 16—Israel is referred to as a harlot woman.

Hosea 2—Israel is referred to as an unfaithful wife.

The Child

From Israel comes a child.

> **REVELATION 12:2**–"Being with child, she cried out in labor and in pain to give birth."

Who is this child?

REVELATION 12:5—"She bore a male Child who was to rule all nations with a rod of iron. And her Child was caught up to God and His throne."

The "rod of iron" is an iron scepter, a symbol of a ruler's authority:

> **Psalm 2:8-9**—"Ask of Me, and I will give You the nations for Your inheritance, and the ends of the earth for Your possession. You shall break them with a rod of iron; You shall dash them to pieces like a potter's vessel."
>
> **Revelation 19:15**—"Now out of His mouth goes a sharp sword, that with it He should strike the nations. And He Himself will rule them with a rod of iron. He Himself treads the winepress of the fierceness and wrath of Almighty God."

The description of the child being "caught up to God" is a reference to Jesus' ascension.

Here, John saw God's redemptive plan for the ages: The nation of Israel, which God created out of nothing, would give birth to the Messiah, Jesus, and through this Child, He would offer salvation to the nations.

But Satan has continually attempted to thwart the redemptive plan of God. He incited antisemitism and is behind Jewish persecutors like Pharaoh, Haman, Herod the Great, Hitler, and radical Islam—but he will never prevail in destroying the Jewish people or the Jewish Messiah.

Israeli Prime Minister Benjamin Netanyahu once spoke about how the nation of Israel has outlasted other world empires, including Babylon, Rome, and the Third Reich, even though Israel has been dispersed and persecuted time after time.[1] God has miraculously brought His people together again and preserved a remnant of them.

The gates of hell will not prevail against the plan of God.

The Dragon

> **REVELATION 12:3**—"Another sign appeared in heaven: behold, a great, fiery red dragon having seven heads and ten horns, and seven diadems on his heads."

Some think this is a picture of the revived Roman Empire, the last world empire. However, the Bible tells us who this is: Satan (Revelation 12:9). Therefore the "seven heads and ten horns, and seven diadems" are simply representative of Satan's authority and his impact on world governments.

Satan also has an impact on the spiritual world, for he drew a third of the angels with him in rebellion against God.

> **REVELATION 12:4**—"His tail drew a third of the stars of heaven and threw them to the earth. And the dragon stood before the woman who was ready to give birth, to devour her Child as soon as it was born."

We do not know how many angels make up a third of the "stars," but even one demon is one too many.

Satan Cast Out

Then Satan fails to stage a coup against God.

> **REVELATION 12:6-8**—"The woman fled into the wilderness, where she has a place prepared by God, that they should feed her there one thousand two hundred and sixty days.
>
> "And war broke out in heaven: Michael and his angels fought with the dragon; and the dragon and his angels fought, but they did not prevail, nor was a place found for them in heaven any longer."

Michael is an archangel fighting on God's side, while Satan is kicked out along with the other angels who rebelled against God.

> **Ezekiel 28:16**—"By the abundance of your trading you became filled with violence within, and you sinned; therefore I cast you as a profane thing out of the mountain of God; and I destroyed you, O covering cherub, from the midst of the fiery stones."
>
> **Luke 10:18**—"He [Jesus] said to them, 'I saw Satan fall like lightning from heaven.'"

Satan's Many Titles

Verses 9 and 10 use many different titles for Satan, but they all refer to the same enemy.

> **REVELATION 12:9-10**—"The great dragon was cast out, that serpent of old, called the Devil and Satan, who deceives the whole world; he was cast to the earth, and his angels were cast out with him.
>
> "Then I heard a loud voice saying in heaven, 'Now salvation, and strength, and the kingdom of our God, and the power of His Christ have come, for the accuser of our brethren, who accused them before our God day and night, has been cast down.'"

Revelation uses various titles for Satan:

1. That serpent of old

In the Hebrew text, the word translated "serpent" is *nāḥāš*, meaning "copper or bronze," so there was something glowing or shining about him.

And it appears that even after being cast out of heaven, Satan still maintains some of his original appearance of light:

> **2 Corinthians 11:14**—"And no wonder! For Satan himself transforms himself into an angel of light."
>
> **Ezekiel 28:13**—"You were in Eden, the garden of God; every precious stone was your covering: the sardius, topaz, and diamond, beryl, onyx, and jasper, sapphire, turquoise, and emerald with gold. The workmanship of your timbrels and pipes was prepared for you on the day you were created."

2. The Devil

The "Devil," *diabolos* in the Greek text, means "accuser."

3. Satan

He is called "Satan"—*satan*, in the Greek text, means "enemy." The devil's intent is to destroy, so we must be watchful.

> **1 Peter 5:8**—"Be sober, be vigilant; because your adversary the devil walks about like a roaring lion, seeking whom he may devour."

4. He who deceives the whole world

Satan will do all he can to deceive people and distract them from the saving knowledge of Jesus.

> **2 Corinthians 4:4**—"...whose minds the god of this age has blinded, who do not believe, lest the light of the gospel of the glory of Christ, who is the image of God, should shine on them."

5. The accuser of our brethren

Revelation 12:10 says Satan accuses us, before God, every day and night relentlessly. He loves to shame and accuse us, but God tells us that Satan is a liar.

Time Is Running Out

A Short Time

Satan will increase the heat against God's people when he knows his time is running short—God will not allow him to roam free for much longer.

> **REVELATION 12:11-12**—"They overcame him by the blood of the Lamb and by the word of their testimony, and they did not love their lives to the death. Therefore rejoice, O heavens, and you who dwell in them! Woe to the inhabitants of the earth and the sea! For the devil has come down to you, having great wrath, because he knows that he has a short time."

The Woman Persecuted

> **REVELATION 12:13-14**—"Now when the dragon saw that he had been cast to the earth, he persecuted the woman who gave birth to the male Child. But the woman was given two wings of a great eagle, that she might fly into the wilderness to her place, where she is nourished for a time and times and half a time, from the presence of the serpent."

Some believe that when the Antichrist reveals himself, Israel will flee into Petra, a city in Jordan, but we do not know this for certain.

Satan Enraged

> **REVELATION 12:15-17**—"So the serpent spewed water out of his mouth like a flood after the woman, that he might cause her to be carried away by the flood. But the earth helped the woman, and the earth opened its mouth and swallowed up the flood which the dragon had spewed out of his mouth.

> And the dragon was enraged with the woman, and he went to make war with the rest of her offspring, who keep the commandments of God and have the testimony of Jesus Christ."

Satan's plan has long been to wipe out God's good works. So when the dragon failed to wipe out Israel, he was even more enraged!

Reflections on Revelation 12

Getting Started

After reading Revelation 12, you might note that the text uses figurative language that draws parallels to the nativity story (Matthew 2), when Jesus could have had John write this chapter in literal terms. What do you think the Bible emphasizes by comparing the persecution of the Christ child at Jesus' first coming to the persecution of Israel before Jesus' second coming (see John 15:18-19; 16:33)?

Study Questions

1. Who is the pregnant woman of Revelation 12:1 (see Genesis 37:9)? What does this tell us about the role of Israel in end-times events (see Romans 11:1-5)?
2. How should we interpret the Bible (see 2 Timothy 2:15)? How can you apply this method of interpretation to your daily devotions?
3. Who is the male Child, and why does He hold a rod of iron (see Revelation 12:2, 5; Psalm 2:8-9; Revelation 19:15)?
4. Who is the dragon (see Revelation 12:3, 9), and why does he hate the woman and Child?
5. The dragon is against the woman and her Child and always has been (Revelation 12:3-4), but God always has a remnant (see Jeremiah 30:11; Romans 11:5). How should this encourage us?
6. Satan still tries to act against the woman despite God's protection of her (see Revelation 12:6-8, 12). What are some modern manifestations of this antisemitic spirit?
7. Satan will deceive the world during the tribulation (Revelation 12:9), but he actively seeks to blind unbelievers'

minds even now (see 2 Corinthians 4:4). What are some examples of how his deception has infiltrated our culture?

8. At some point, Israel will be forced to flee (Revelation 12:13-14), but God already has a plan to nourish His people. What does this pre-planned rescue say about the nature of our Father (see Acts 14:17)?
9. Why is Satan so enraged by the end of the chapter (Revelation 12:15-17)? How are the saints able to triumph even over the rage of the enemy (see Deuteronomy 32:43; 1 John 4:4; Revelation 12:11)?

Important Takeaways for Us Today

1. Satan is the enemy of our souls, and we need to be acquainted with his ways to know how to combat them. Describe how each of the enemy's titles detail one of his tactics and how you combat these tactics.
    a. That serpent of old (see Ezekiel 28:13; 2 Corinthians 11:14; Galatians 1:8-9)
    b. The devil (see Ephesians 6:11; Jude 1:9)
    c. Satan (see 1 Peter 5:8-9)
    d. He who deceives the whole world (see 2 Corinthians 4:4; 1 John 4:1)
    e. The accuser of our brethren (see Revelation 12:10)

2. Jesus is called the "male Child who was to rule all nations with a rod of iron" (Revelation 12:5), a title emphasizing His status as the Son of David, King of kings, and Judge of all the earth. Why do you think God chooses to emphasize these aspects of Christ set against the context of the temporary rule of the god of this world (see Isaiah 14:16-17; 2 Thessalonians 2:8; 1 John 5:5)?

13

The Two Beasts

REVELATION 13

Do you know who the Antichrist is? Christians throughout time have wondered about the Antichrist's identity and have imagined him to be Nero, Hitler, Stalin, maybe the Pope, or the leader of the United Nations. But no one has ruled the globe as Revelation prophesies the Antichrist will do. Some Christians have also thought they knew what the mark of the beast was, claiming it to be a barcode or a credit card chip. But rather than reading the world into Revelation, let us see what the Bible says about these topics.

The Beast from the Sea

The Antichrist

The Antichrist is not referred to as such in Revelation; instead, here he is called the beast 28 times. In fact, the only books in the Bible that use the term *antichrist* are 1 and 2 John: four times in 1 John, and two times in 2 John.

The Antichrist is the first beast, the one who will rise from the water, according to the start of John's vision in Revelation 13.

> **REVELATION 13:1**—"I stood on the sand of the sea. And I saw a beast rising up out of the sea, having seven heads and ten horns, and on his horns ten crowns, and on his heads a blasphemous name."

This beast is different from the second beast, the beast from the earth, because he is the Antichrist who will become a global, political dictator, while the second is the False Prophet, who will become a global, religious leader.

The Spirit of Antichrist

While there will be only one Antichrist, there are many powerful people throughout history who were inspired by Satan to rebel against God and His people, thus possessing the spirit of Antichrist. They were antichrists (lowercase *a* antichrists, but not the Antichrist himself):

> **1 John 2:18**—"Little children, it is the last hour; and as you have heard that the Antichrist is coming, even now many antichrists have come, by which we know that it is the last hour."

Consider Roman Emperor Nero, who would dip Christians in tar and light them as human torches to illuminate his gardens. He was an antichrist, one of many.

Preterist View

Those who hold this view say that Revelation is history rather than prophecy, and they believe that the Antichrist was Nero.

There have been many other possible Antichrists put forth by the church. Some evangelicals in the late 1930s believed Hitler was the Antichrist and Mussolini his False Prophet. Mao, the greatest mass murderer of all time, killed an estimated 40 million of his own people.[1] But he was an antichrist, not *the* Antichrist. Idi Amin, the Butcher of Uganda, was another lowercase *a* antichrist.

There are many antichrists, but only one will be a global dictator, which the Bible refers to as the Antichrist.

Characteristics of Antichrist

1. He will speak blasphemies

> **Daniel 11:36a**—"The king shall do according to his own will: he shall exalt and magnify himself above every god, shall speak blasphemies against the God of gods."

> **REVELATION 13:6**–"He opened his mouth in blasphemy against God, to blaspheme His name, His tabernacle, and those who dwell in heaven."

2. He will hold power till the end of the tribulation

> **Daniel 11:36b**—"[He] shall prosper till the wrath has been accomplished; for what has been determined shall be done." The "wrath" here is the tribulation.

3. He will have no regard for the God of his fathers

> **Daniel 11:37a**—"He shall regard neither the God of his fathers…"

The NIV and ESV Bibles say "gods" rather than "God," but the Hebrew word is *Elohim*, a plural description for the triune God of the Bible. This phrase is likely an idiom indicating that the Antichrist is Jewish.

4. He will have no regard for the desire of women

> **Daniel 11:37b**—"…nor the desire of women, nor regard any god; for he shall exalt himself above them all."

Some interpret this to mean that the Antichrist will be a homosexual, but again, this is a Jewish idiom. The "desire of women" is code for the Messiah. Every young woman of that day hoped to be God's chosen vessel for giving birth to the Messiah—the desire of women. Of course, it was God's providential will, in His providential timing, to choose Mary of Nazareth.

5. He will honor a god of fortresses

> **Daniel 11:38-39**—"In their place he shall honor a god of fortresses; and a god which his fathers did not know he shall honor with gold and silver, with precious stones and pleasant things. Thus he shall act against the strongest fortresses with a foreign god, which he shall acknowledge, and advance its glory; and he shall cause them to rule over many, and divide the land for gain."

That is, the Antichrist will hold unilateral power and use military force to subdue the people of the world. And when the world is divided into ten geographical territories, they will cede power over to the Antichrist. Revelation 17 calls them the "ten horns."

> **REVELATION 17:12-13**–"The ten horns which you saw are ten kings who have received no kingdom as yet, but they receive authority for one hour as kings with the beast. These are of one mind, and they will give their power and authority to the beast."

We can see some of this world tension and division of power even now within the European Union and Brexit. Perhaps because of economic or health reasons, our liberties will dwindle. Think of how quickly COVID increased government control and decreased personal liberties! It will not take much for combined government entities to seize power and control citizens.

Satan's Tool

> **REVELATION 13:2**–"Now the beast which I saw was like a leopard, his feet were like the feet of a bear, and his mouth like the mouth of a lion. The dragon gave him his power, his throne, and great authority."

Satan, the dragon, will give the Antichrist his power, but in the end, the Antichrist will simply be a convenient tool.

Mortal Wound

> **REVELATION 13:3**–"I saw one of his heads as if it had been mortally wounded, and his deadly wound was healed. And all the world marveled and followed the beast."

It seems apparent that the foolish shepherd, the Antichrist, will sustain injuries from an assassination attempt.

> **Zechariah 11:15-17**—"The Lord said to me, 'Next, take for yourself the implements of a foolish shepherd. For indeed I will raise up a shepherd in the land who will not care for those who are cut off, nor seek the young, nor heal those that are broken, nor feed those that still stand. But he will eat the flesh of the fat and tear their hooves in pieces.
>
> "Woe to the worthless shepherd, who leaves the flock! A sword shall be against his arm and against his right eye; his arm shall completely wither, and his right eye shall be totally blinded.'"

Perhaps the injury will damage the left side of the Antichrist's brain, resulting in limited use of his right eye and right arm. The muscles in his arm will atrophy. We do not know the specifics, but what we do know is that the damage will be great enough that, when he recovers through the False Prophet's counterfeit miracle, people everywhere—in awe—will worship him as a god.

Idolatrous Worship

> **REVELATION 13:4**–"They worshiped the dragon who gave authority to the beast; and they worshiped the beast, saying, 'Who is like the beast? Who is able to make war with him?'"

People will start worshipping Satan. And the False Prophet will point these people further into this idolatry.

> **REVELATION 13:5**–"He was given a mouth speaking great things and blasphemies, and he was given authority to continue for forty-two months."

That refers to the second half of the tribulation period. The Antichrist will operate as a pseudo god for three-and-a-half years.

Saints Persecuted

> **REVELATION 13:7**–"It was granted to him to make war with the saints and to overcome them. And authority was given him over every tribe, tongue, and nation."

The "saints," or the tribulation Christians, will be persecuted. But not for long.

> **REVELATION 13:8-10**–"All who dwell on the earth will worship him, whose names have not been written in the Book of Life of the Lamb slain from the foundation of the world.

> "If anyone has an ear, let him hear. He who leads into captivity shall go into captivity; he who kills with the sword must be killed with the sword. Here is the patience and the faith of the saints."

The Beast from the Earth

The False Prophet

> **REVELATION 13:11**–"I saw another beast coming up out of the earth, and he had two horns like a lamb and spoke like a dragon."

While the Antichrist emerges from the sea of people, the False Prophet emerges from the worldly systems of the earth.

The False Prophet has two horns, for two is the number for testimony—in his case, false testimony—and he is like a lamb because the testimony is religious in nature. However, though he appears like a lamb, he speaks like a dragon because Satan is behind him.

The False Prophet is duplicitous. He is not what he seems.

His Purpose

> **REVELATION 13:12**–"He exercises all the authority of the first beast in his presence, and causes the earth and those who dwell in it to worship the first beast, whose deadly wound was healed."

The False Prophet's job is to promote the Antichrist, and he will likely be involved in the healing of the Antichrist's deadly wound because he can perform counterfeit miracles.

His Power

> **REVELATION 13:13**—"He performs great signs, so that he even makes fire come down from heaven on the earth in the sight of men."

The False Prophet mimics Elijah the prophet as part of his deception. Do not embrace everything that looks miraculous! We must "test the spirits," test manifestations, to see "whether they are of God" (1 John 4:1).

We all have a fascination with the supernatural, but do not let your fascination cause you to believe that everything that appears supernatural is from the Lord. We must test everything against the Scriptures and run from what is contrary to God's Word.

His Deception

> **REVELATION 13:14-15**—"He deceives those who dwell on the earth by those signs which he was granted to do in the sight of the beast, telling those who dwell on the earth to make an image to the beast who was wounded by the sword and lived. He was granted power to give breath to the image of the beast, that the image of the beast should both speak and cause as many as would not worship the image of the beast to be killed."

See the false religiosity? The False Prophet directs people to the Antichrist and away from God, and further, he persecutes the people of God.

He also orders that an image of the Antichrist be set up in the temple and gives life to it. Some believe this image is the personage of the Antichrist, who then goes into the temple as is detailed in 2 Thessalonians 2:4. Others believe that this image is not the Antichrist, but an exact replica of him, perhaps a statue of some kind, or a hologram, or a digital appearance of the Antichrist created with the use of artificial intelligence.

And the kind of "life" given to this image is not *bio* but *pneuma*, meaning "breath, spirit, or soul." There is a supernatural, spiritual force at work here.

Either way, this passage tells us that God will be blasphemed when the image is set up in the temple of God. Jesus refers to this blasphemy in Matthew 24:15. This tells us that a Jewish temple will be built on the Temple Mount sometime in the future, for there has not been a temple since AD 70.

> **REVELATION 13:16-17**—"He causes all, both small and great, rich and poor, free and slave, to receive a mark on their right hand or on their foreheads, and that no one may buy or sell except one who has the mark or the name of the beast, or the number of his name."

The False Prophet, besides persecuting the saints and encouraging idolatrous worship of the Antichrist, also causes all to take the mark of the beast as a prerequisite to buy and sell. But Christians (those who become believers after the rapture and during the tribulation) will refuse, meaning that they will probably starve because they can neither acquire food and other necessities, nor earn a living. And if they do not starve to death, they will likely be martyred for their faith.

The good news is that these believers are going to heaven regardless of what they face on Earth for refusing to take the mark.

> **REVELATION 13:18**—"Here is wisdom. Let him who has understanding calculate the number of the beast, for it is the number of a man: His number is 666."

The number for the Antichrist is 666. The number six in the Bible is the number for man because God created us on the sixth day. The triple use of six could simply be referring to mankind because the Antichrist rises from humanity. But it could also refer to the unholy trinity: Satan, the Antichrist, and the False Prophet.

But we cannot be sure about what the number 666 itself refers to, or to whom it refers.

Christians used to think credit cards and barcodes were the mark of the beast. Some later thought Ronald Wilson Reagan was the Antichrist because his first, middle, and last names each have six letters. People who have way too much time on their hands are coming up with this stuff! Do not believe it!

People make many guesses, but you know what? If you believe in the pretribulation view of the rapture as I do, we will not be here when the mark of the beast is given out. The church will be gone—that is the hope of the church.

> **1 Thessalonians 5:4-9**—"You, brethren, are not in darkness, so that this Day should overtake you as a thief. You are all sons of light and sons of the day. We are not of the night nor of darkness. Therefore let us not sleep, as others do, but let us watch and be sober. For those who sleep, sleep at night, and those who get drunk are drunk at night. But let us who are of the day be sober, putting on the breastplate of faith and love, and as a helmet the hope of salvation. For God did not appoint us to wrath, but to obtain salvation through our Lord Jesus Christ."

Reflections on Revelation 13

Getting Started

Revelation 13 covers the rise of the two beasts—the Antichrist and the False Prophet. This rise in their power includes blasphemies against God, idolatrous worship, and the persecution of the saints. Why do you think God will allow the rise of so much evil? Why does He allow evil (though restrained) even today (see Judges 2:21-22; Matthew 13:24-30, 36-43; Romans 8:28; 9:22)?

Study Questions

1. What does the Antichrist coming from the sea symbolize (Revelation 13:1)? In what ways is he the antithesis of Christ (see John 3:16; 15:13; Philippians 2:5-8; 2 Thessalonians 2:4; Revelation 13:7)?
2. What is the difference between the spirit of antichrist and the Antichrist (see 1 John 2:18, 22; 4:3; 2 John 1:7)? How can we be led by God rather than influenced by Satan (see Matthew 16:15-24; Galatians 5:16; Colossians 3:2-3)?
3. The Antichrist will speak blasphemies against God and all that is sacred (see Daniel 11:36; Revelation 13:6). What root sin does the Antichrist's boasting point to (see Proverbs 8:13; Daniel 11:36), and what does God want from us instead (see Psalm 34:18; Ecclesiastes 5:2)?
4. The Bible says the Antichrist will not regard the God of his fathers (see Daniel 11:37). What does this phrase most likely indicate about the Antichrist's heritage? How does this add context to the deception that falls on the Jews and the desecration of the temple (see Daniel 9:27)?
5. What does the phrase "the desire of women" mean, and what

does the Antichrist choose instead of having regard for the desire of women (see Daniel 11:37-39)?

6. What might drive the ten kings of Revelation 17:12-13 to give their power over to the beast? How have you seen this push toward globalism in our culture?
7. How do the Antichrist's grievous injuries lead people to idolize him (see Zechariah 11:17; Revelation 13:3)? How should this serve as a warning to us (see Exodus 7:8-12; Matthew 7:22-23; 2 Thessalonians 2:9)?
8. The beast will have power to persecute the saints, but Revelation 13:10 ends with a note of hope. What is the saints' hope (Revelation 13:7-10)?
9. Why does the False Prophet emerge from the earth (Revelation 13:11)? What characterizes the earthly system he emerges from (see 1 Corinthians 7:31; 1 John 2:15-17)?
10. Why does the False Prophet look like a lamb and speak like a dragon (Revelation 13:11)? What does this description tell you about how false prophets deceive people (see Matthew 7:15-20; 2 Corinthians 11:13-15, 2 Peter 2:1; Jude 1:4)?

Important Takeaways for Us Today

1. Knowing that Satan can create counterfeit miracles (Revelation 13:2-3), how are we to test the spirits to know whether a sign is from God or the enemy (see Deuteronomy 18:22; Matthew 7:15-16; Luke 6:43-45; Acts 17:11; 1 John 4:1-6)?
2. Revelation 13:14-15 describes the False Prophet giving life to the image of the beast. This will be a cheap imitation of God's creative power, yet people will end up worshipping this image just as they worshipped the Antichrist, a corrupted form of God's image bearers. Knowing this, answer the following:

a. Why do you think people choose to worship lesser things rather than God (see Matthew 6:24; 7:13-14; 19:20-26; John 3:19; 2 Timothy 4:3-5)?

b. Why have you chosen lesser things in the past?

14

Protected from Wrath

REVELATION 14

If you are wondering how any Christian is going to survive the tribulation, Revelation 14 is your answer: God will preserve a remnant as He always has, except this time, He will specifically give the 144,000 a seal of protection. But who are the 144,000? What are they being protected from? And what is the climactic battle that comes at the end of this chapter? Let us look at John's visions to answer these questions.

Context

Parenthetical Chapter

Revelation 14 is another parenthetical chapter out of chronological order, perhaps to insert hope and God's mercy after such heavy chapters about the Antichrist and the horrors of the tribulation.

Stage Set for Globalism

Secular philosophy is already leading us toward the globalist setting like that seen in Revelation 13. And when people say "your truth" or "my truth," they are subscribing to this relativistic philosophy.

Jan Tinbergen, a Nobel Prize–winning Dutch economist, said, "Mankind's problems can no longer be solved by national governments. What is needed is world government."[1]

In a speech given in 2013, Hillary Clinton said, "My dream is a hemispheric common market, with open trade and open borders, sometime in the future..."[2]

Preview of Jesus' Return

Three Visions

Revelation 14 includes three visions that God showed John. In verse 1, John said, "Then I looked," introducing the vision of the 144,000 whom God sealed. In verse 6, John said, "Then I saw," introducing a vision of three angels. In verse 14, John said, "Then I looked," introducing a vision of believers separated from nonbelievers. But though our Bibles use different words, "saw" and "looked" are the same word in the Greek text.

The Lamb

> **REVELATION 14:1**—"Then I looked, and behold, a Lamb standing on Mount Zion, and with Him one hundred and forty-four thousand, having His Father's name written on their foreheads."

Jesus is referred to as the Lamb 26 times in Revelation. It is His most cherished title for Himself. He opts to present Himself primarily as the atoning sacrifice for the sins of the world.

Mount Zion

Chapter 14 starts with "then I looked." Some believe John was looking at a scene in heaven, but others believe he was literally on Mount Zion.

I believe this is a literal picture of Jerusalem. First, because in the next verse, John said he heard a voice from heaven, and it seems unlikely he would specify where the voice came from if he were in the same location as the voice.

> **REVELATION 14:2**–"I heard a voice from heaven, like the voice of many waters, and like the voice of loud thunder. And I heard the sound of harpists playing their harps."

Second, because Mount Zion refers to the hill of Jerusalem 160 times throughout Scripture, and every time, except twice, it refers to the literal Jerusalem in Israel.

Jesus on Mount Zion

Jesus is seen "standing on Mount Zion" (Revelation 14:1), which is a preview of Jesus' second coming. His return is further outlined in Revelation 19, which says He will come to Mount Zion after the seven-year tribulation and the victory that follows at Armageddon.

The 144,000

> **REVELATION 14:3**–"They sang as it were a new song before the throne, before the four living creatures, and the elders; and no one could learn that song except the hundred and forty-four thousand who were redeemed from the earth."

These are the 144,000 Jews whom God sealed in chapter 7, and who bear the name of God on their foreheads.

> **Revelation** 7:3—"Saying, 'Do not harm the earth, the sea, or the trees till we have sealed the servants of our God on their foreheads.'"

These are Jews who put their faith and trust in Jesus as Messiah, and God protects them and uses them to evangelize to the world.

Characteristics of the 144,000

The Bible gives us five characteristics of those who will be part of the 144,000.

1. They are virgins

> **REVELATION 14:4a**–"These are the ones who were not defiled with women, for they are virgins."

Some argue from this passage that the 144,000 are literally male virgins, but I lean toward the figurative explanation because virginity is often used in Scripture to indicate those who are set apart for God.

> **Isaiah 37:22**—"This is the word which the LORD has spoken concerning him: 'The virgin, the daughter of Zion, has despised you, laughed you to scorn; the daughter of Jerusalem has shaken her head behind your back!'"

> **2 Corinthians 11:2**—"I am jealous for you with godly jealousy. For I have betrothed you to one husband, that I may present you as a chaste virgin to Christ."

Therefore, verse 4 is probably referring to the 144,000 as "virgins" to describe their pure hearts and devotion to God.

2. They follow the Lamb

> **REVELATION 14:4b**–"These are the ones who follow the Lamb wherever He goes."

They are attentive and obedient to the Lord Jesus.

3. They are the redeemed from among men

> **REVELATION 14:4c**—"These were redeemed from among men, being firstfruits to God and to the Lamb."

This phrase indicates that they were bought and freed by God from among the sea of humanity.

4. They speak no deceit

> **REVELATION 14:5a**—"In their mouth was found no deceit."

They were not compromising with their words or deceiving with their speech. There was no lying on their lips. They spoke with truth and integrity.

5. They stand faultless

> **REVELATION 14:5b**—"They are without fault before the throne of God."

This does not mean that they were sinless, but that they were living their lives under the power of God and walking in Him.

> **Jude 1:24**—"Now to Him who is able to keep you from stumbling, and to present you faultless before the presence of His glory with exceeding joy."

Proclamations of Angels

First Angel

Each of the three angels in John's vision has his own task. The first angel evangelizes the nations.

> **REVELATION 14:6-7**—"I saw another angel flying in the midst of heaven, having the everlasting gospel to preach to those who dwell on the earth—to every nation, tribe, tongue, and people—saying with a loud voice, 'Fear God and give glory to Him, for the hour of His judgment has come; and worship Him who made heaven and earth, the sea and springs of water.'"

This is the first and only time that God will use an angel rather than people to preach the gospel. This is likely because, at this time, the church has been raptured and the tribulation saints are getting martyred. Thus, God uses an angel to fill the role of an evangelist. And the angel preaches to "every nation," so either the gospel is translated midair, or he goes around the world and takes turns evangelizing different people in their own languages.

This is a wonderful miracle. The tribulation is a horrible time, and by chapter 14, half the world's population is gone. Thus, Revelation is a book that some people have a hard time reading because it presents God as a vengeful Judge. Yet in this chapter, God's heart for saving people is clearly seen by the way that He dispatches an angel to circle the world and preach the Word.

Second Angel

> **REVELATION 14:8**—"Another angel followed, saying, 'Babylon is fallen, is fallen, that great city, because she has made all nations drink of the wine of the wrath of her fornication.'"

This second angel declares the coming downfall of the global, worldly system.

Third Angel

The third angel declares condemnation to those who take the mark of the beast.

> **REVELATION 14:9-11**—"A third angel followed them, saying with a loud voice, 'If anyone worships the beast and his image, and receives his mark on his forehead or on his hand, he himself shall also drink of the wine of the wrath of God, which is poured out full strength into the cup of His indignation. He shall be tormented with fire and brimstone in the presence of the holy angels and in the presence of the Lamb. And the smoke of their torment ascends forever and ever; and they have no rest day or night, who worship the beast and his image, and whoever receives the mark of his name.'"

The Saints

A Remnant

> **REVELATION 14:12**—"Here is the patience of the saints; here are those who keep the commandments of God and the faith of Jesus."

Despite how bleak this condemnation is, God reminds us that even during the tribulation period, there will be a remnant.

Blessed Dead

Some of the remnant will die as martyrs, but death is not the end:

> **REVELATION 14:13**—"I heard a voice from heaven saying to me, 'Write: "Blessed are the dead who die in the Lord from now on."' 'Yes,' says the Spirit, 'that they may rest from their labors, and their works follow them.'"

Death is ultimately rest for believers, whose good works will be rewarded.

Reaping the Earth's Harvest

Son of Man

REVELATION 14:14–"Then I looked, and behold, a white cloud, and on the cloud sat One like the Son of Man, having on His head a golden crown, and in His hand a sharp sickle."

"One like the Son of Man" is a reference to Jesus, who is figuratively the harvester of the earth. Jesus will harvest men's souls, separating the saved from the lost.

The "golden crown" depicts victory, and the "sharp sickle" is a picture of authority.

Harvest Announced

REVELATION 14:15–"Another angel came out of the temple, crying with a loud voice to Him who sat on the cloud, 'Thrust in Your sickle and reap, for the time has come for You to reap, for the harvest of the earth is ripe.'"

This angel pleads with Jesus to start reaping, saying that the earth is ready for reaping, and Jesus does:

REVELATION 14:16–"So He who sat on the cloud thrust in His sickle on the earth, and the earth was reaped."

The Reaping

Angel number two gets deployed, and he also has a sharp sickle.

REVELATION 14:17–"Another angel came out of the temple which is in heaven, he also having a sharp sickle."

Then angel number three tells angel number two to start gathering unbelievers for judgment, and angel number two begins reaping till blood covers the streets:

> **REVELATION 14:18-20**—"Another angel came out from the altar, who had power over fire, and he cried with a loud cry to him who had the sharp sickle, saying, 'Thrust in your sharp sickle and gather the clusters of the vine of the earth, for her grapes are fully ripe.' So the angel thrust his sickle into the earth and gathered the vine of the earth, and threw it into the great winepress of the wrath of God. And the winepress was trampled outside the city, and blood came out of the winepress, up to the horses' bridles, for one thousand six hundred furlongs."

The tribulation will conclude with the climactic battle of Armageddon (from the Hebrew *har məgiddô*, meaning "the mountain of Megiddo"). This battle will take place near Mount Megiddo in the Jezreel Valley of Israel, where all the nations will gather to wage war against Israel and the God of Israel.

Interestingly, Napolean went to Megiddo and said, "There is no place in the whole world more suited for war than this...[It is] the most natural battleground of the whole earth."[3] It sure will be a battlefield! Blood will flow down from the Jezreel Valley to the Kidron Valley alongside Jerusalem. "Kidron" is derived from a word in Hebrew that means "black" because the valley often ran black with the blood of the slaughtered sacrificial lambs. When Jesus comes to judge, the Bible says that the blood will flow for 1,600 furlongs (or "1,600 stadia" in the NIV), which in today's measurements would be 180 miles. Now, because this is a long distance for blood to flow and Israel itself is only about 290 miles, it is likely that this number is figurative.

Jesus prophesied regarding this battle in Matthew 13:36-43, where He said that, at the end of the age, He will use angels to separate the wheat from the tares. This picture of the separation of the wheat (the righteous) from the tares (the unrighteous) is echoed in Revelation and will be fulfilled in the end times. But until the head forms with its kernels, you cannot tell whether the plants are wheat or tares, so Jesus will withhold from reaping until the end.

May we be ready for Jesus' return.

Reflections on Revelation 14

Getting Started

Compare the titles and roles of Jesus in the beginning and at the end of the chapter (Revelation 14:1, 4, 14-16), as well as in the first and the third angel proclamations (Revelation 14:6-7, 9-11). What do these contrasts tell us about the character of our God (see Exodus 34:5-7)? What is our responsibility in this dynamic (see Genesis 4:7)?

Study Questions

1. How is secular philosophy setting the stage for a global government? What are we as believers to use to inform our perspective instead of secular philosophy (see Romans 12:2; 1 Corinthians 2:14-16; 1 Timothy 6:20-21)?
2. How did Jesus present Himself in the first vision of Revelation 14 (see verse 1)? What is the significance of Jesus presenting Himself primarily as the Lamb in Revelation?
3. Revelation 14:1 is about Jesus sealing the 144,000. How does this contrast with the mark unbelievers receive (see Revelation 13:16-18; 14:9-11)?
4. Why do you think Jesus sealed the 144,000 of Revelation 14:3? What does this tell us about God's heart toward man?
5. What are the five characteristics of the 144,000 (see Revelation 14:4-5; 2 Corinthians 11:2; Jude 1:24)? How are they able to stand faultless despite being men with the same sinful nature as everyone else (see Romans 3:21-26)?
6. In the vision of the three angels, John wrote that the job of the first angel is to evangelize to the nations (Revelation 14:6-7). What makes this method of evangelization unique and necessary?

7. What is the second angel's proclamation, and what sin brought this on (Revelation 14:8)? In what way does Babylon's sin manifest (see Jeremiah 3:1-3; Hosea 1:2)?
8. What is the proclamation of the third angel, according to Revelation 14:9-11, and how does it pair with the proclamation of the first angel in Revelation 14:6-7 (see Deuteronomy 30:19; Joshua 24:15)?
9. Why does Revelation 14:13 call the martyrs the blessed dead and describe their deaths as rest? How should this promise change how we view death (see Philippians 1:21; 1 Thessalonians 4:13-14)?
10. What does Jesus' sickle and the reaping at the end of chapter 14 represent (see verses 15-20)? Why should believers not be afraid of this end-times judgment (see Matthew 13:36-43; 1 Thessalonians 5:9)?

Important Takeaways for Us Today

1. What is Jesus' standing on Mount Zion in Revelation 14:1 a preview of, and how does this bring hope to believers?
2. Only the 144,000 believers of Revelation 14:3 could hear the song of heaven sung in verse 2. What is a song that God sung to you amid a dry season (see Psalms 40:3; 42:8; Isaiah 42:10), and how was it helpful to you?

15

Rejoicing in Heaven

REVELATION 15

This is a short chapter that packs a punch. Though Revelation 15 only has eight verses, the number "seven" is repeated eight times. In the Bible, seven is the number for completion, and here, it emphasizes that the prophecy is coming to an end. As you read, remember that this is a temporary reprieve, for after this chapter we will soon move on to God's bowl judgments, which come in quick succession.

Prelude to the Bowl Judgments

The End Predicted

> **REVELATION 15:1**—"I saw another sign in heaven, great and marvelous: seven angels having the seven last plagues, for in them the wrath of God is complete."

The phrase "I saw another sign in heaven" indicates John was having another vision, though this time, it was set in heaven.

The frequent mention of "seven" within eight verses indicates that the tribulation will soon be completed. God is giving a glimpse that the end is near. These are the "seven last plagues," after all, and "in them the wrath of God is complete."

The word "complete," in the original Greek language, is *tetelestai*. It was a word used with different applications. For example, it was an accounting term written on an invoice whenever a debt was paid in full—*tetelestai*. It was also a word that was written across a prison door when a criminal's sentence was completed—*tetelestai*.

And it is the same Greek word Jesus uttered from the cross when He said, "It is finished" (John 19:30). Jesus meant that He had finished the whole redemptive work for mankind on the cross.

And in this passage in Revelation, the word speaks of God's wrath coming to an end or completion—*tetelestai*.

This is a good reminder that God's wrath does not last forever. As the psalmist wrote:

> **Psalm 85:5-9**—"Will You be angry with us forever? Will You prolong Your anger to all generations? Will You not revive us again, that Your people may rejoice in You? Show us Your mercy, Lord, and grant us Your salvation.
>
> "I will hear what God the Lord will speak, for He will speak peace to His people and to His saints; but let them not turn back to folly. Surely His salvation is near to those who fear Him, that glory may dwell in our land."

Sea of Humanity

> **REVELATION 15:2a**–"I saw something like a sea of glass mingled with fire."

The word "like" reminds us this is not a literal sea, but something similar. Again, "sea" almost never means a body of water in Revelation, but rather, a vast number of people, like it does here. And this "sea" is mingled with fire, which is an indication of judgment.

Victorious Saints

> **REVELATION 15:2b**–"[I saw] those who have the victory over the beast, over his image and over his mark and over the number of his name, standing on the sea of glass, having harps of God."

John saw the martyred tribulation saints, a glorious picture of our hope. The beast will have many saints killed, but despite their deaths, they overcame him through the blood of the Lamb. And it looks like there might be something to the popular depiction of people playing harps in heaven!

Heavenly Songs

> **REVELATION 15:3-4**–"They sing the song of Moses, the servant of God, and the song of the Lamb, saying:
>
> > "Great and marvelous are Your works, Lord God Almighty! Just and true are Your ways, O King of the saints! Who shall not fear You, O Lord, and glorify Your name? For You alone are holy. For all nations shall come and worship before You, for Your judgments have been manifested."

These victorious saints sing the songs of Moses and the Lamb, as if in perfect combination of law and grace. These songs are glorifying God's works, ways, and worth.

Another Vision

> **REVELATION 15:5**–"After these things I looked, and behold, the temple of the tabernacle of the testimony in heaven was opened."

"I looked" indicates yet another vision.

Seven Angels

> **REVELATION 15:6**—"Out of the temple came the seven angels having the seven plagues, clothed in pure bright linen, and having their chests girded with golden bands."

These seven angelic creatures coming out of the place of holiness are about to distribute the plagues God has assigned to them.

Seven Bowls

> **REVELATION 15:7-8**—"One of the four living creatures gave to the seven angels seven golden bowls full of the wrath of God who lives forever and ever. The temple was filled with smoke from the glory of God and from His power, and no one was able to enter the temple till the seven plagues of the seven angels were completed."

These seven bowls are probably like the golden incense bowls that the priests used in their temple service.

Four Living Creatures

The four living creatures of Revelation 15:7 are mentioned in Revelation 4. Again, they are angelic beings, and they surround the throne of God. These four creatures were entrusted to assign the plagues to the seven angels.

Reflections on Revelation 15

Getting Started

Revelation 15:3-4 shows the saints singing of God's mercy and wrath. How does that form an outline for the rest of the chapter (see Revelation 15:2, 7-8)?

Study Questions

1. Why does Revelation 15:1 use *tetelestai* for the word "complete," the same word Christ used on the cross (see John 19:30)?
2. Why does Revelation 15 emphasize the number seven? Why should this symbolism help us approach God with confidence (see Psalm 85:5-9; Isaiah 1:18; Hebrews 4:16)?
3. Revelation 15:2 describes "something like a sea of glass mingled with fire." What does this simile signify, and what does this image illustrate about God's patience (see Romans 2:4-5; Galatians 6:7; 2 Peter 3:9-10)?
4. Though the saints are part of the "sea" of humanity, they are seen "standing on the sea of glass" (Revelation 15:2), victorious over their enemies. What gave these saints—and gives us—this victory (see Romans 8:31, 35-37; 1 Corinthians 15:57)?
5. What do the songs of Moses and the Lamb represent (Revelation 15:3-4)? How are both aspects met in the person of Jesus (Romans 3:21-26)?
6. What do the saints praise God for in their songs (see Revelation 7:9-10; 15:3-4)? How do your experiences shape your songs of praise (see Exodus 15:1-5; Judges 5:1-2; Psalm 126:2)?

7. When the seven angels come out of the holy temple of God, what are they coming out to do (Revelation 15:5-6)? What does this teach us about the nature of holiness (see Exodus 33:20; Psalm 96:9; Isaiah 6:1-7)? How should we live in light of this truth (see 1 Peter 1:15-17)?
8. What are the seven incense bowls of Revelation 15:7-8, and what do they represent (see Psalm 141:1-2; Malachi 1:11; Revelation 5:8)? As believers, how often are we to offer incense (see Luke 18:1; Colossians 4:2; 1 Thessalonians 5:17)? What does this tell you about the kind of relationship God wishes to have with us (see Romans 8:32; Galatians 4:6-7; James 4:8)?
9. How do the saints' prayers and God's response in Revelation 15:7-8 parallel the scene of Revelation 8:3-5? What do these parallels teach us about prayer (see James 5:16)?

Important Takeaways for Us Today

1. One way the saints can stand is by "having harps of God" (Revelation 15:2). What is one way God has used worship to help you overcome—for example, as happened to Paul and Silas in Acts 16:18-26?
2. In Revelation 15:2, the saints gain victory over the beast, his image, and his mark. In what ways do believers today overcome the temptations that are in our world, according to…

    a. Ephesians 6:11-18?

    b. Colossians 3:5-10?

    c. 2 Corinthians 1:22 and Ephesians 4:30?

16

Torment on Earth

REVELATION 16

These last days of the tribulation involve plagues of sores, rivers of blood, and a scorching sun. Throughout this trouble, it is easy to miss the blessing couched within the curses. Yet the Lord calls us to hope, for even those who were not prepared for the rapture may still be saved during this time and prepare themselves for Jesus' second coming. As Jesus says in Revelation 16:15, "Behold, I am coming as a thief. Blessed is he who watches, and keeps his garments, lest he walk naked and they see his shame." Amen!

The Seven Bowls

First Bowl

REVELATION 16:1-2—"I heard a loud voice from the temple saying to the seven angels, 'Go and pour out the bowls of the wrath of God on the earth.'

> "So the first went and poured out his bowl upon the earth, and a foul and loathsome sore came upon the men who had the mark of the beast and those who worshiped his image."

This is like the sixth plague of Egypt, when boils broke out on people. Some historians look at the words "foul and loathsome sore" and think there is something malignant behind the sores, perhaps because of the mark of the beast that people have had placed on their foreheads or right hands. Either way, they will earn God's selective judgment.

Second Bowl

> **REVELATION 16:3**—"The second angel poured out his bowl on the sea, and it became blood as of a dead man; and every living creature in the sea died."

This is like the second trumpet judgment, during which a third of the sea becomes blood. But now, all the seas become blood. Imagine what this judgment will be like for those living on Earth at that time: since the seas turn to blood and every creature within dies, a large food source vanishes, and a horrible stench rises.

Third Bowl

> **REVELATION 16:4**—"The third angel poured out his bowl on the rivers and springs of water, and they became blood."

Seventy percent of Earth's surface is covered by water, but 97 percent of that is salt water and only 3 percent is fresh water. However, most of that 3 percent of freshwater is locked in the polar ice caps and glaciers. Thus, all of humanity currently survives on less than 1 percent of Earth's water. Consider how fragile our freshwater supply is when the entire world population is dependent upon less than 1 percent of Earth's total water mass.

This bowl judgment pollutes freshwater sources and makes drinkable water impossible to find.

Blood for Blood

The angel of the waters affirms the justice of God in executing judgment, calling out the hateful way unbelievers have persecuted God's prophets.

> **REVELATION 16:5-7**—"I heard the angel of the waters saying:
>
> > "'You are righteous, O Lord, the One who is and who was and who is to be, because You have judged these things. For they have shed the blood of saints and prophets, and You have given them blood to drink. For it is their just due.'
>
> "And I heard another from the altar saying, 'Even so, Lord God Almighty, true and righteous are Your judgments.'"

Fourth Bowl

With the fourth bowl, God ramps up the intensity of the sun enough to scorch men, and there's not enough sunscreen that will save anyone then.

> **REVELATION 16:8**—"The fourth angel poured out his bowl on the sun, and power was given to him to scorch men with fire."

> **Isaiah 30:26**—"Moreover the light of the moon will be as the light of the sun, and the light of the sun will be sevenfold, as the light of seven days, in the day that the LORD binds up the bruise of His people and heals the stroke of their wound."

In *The Revelation Record*, Dr. Henry Morris (a former department chair of civil engineering at Virginia Tech) calculated the effects on the planet if the sun's heat were intensified by seven times. He concluded that the great ice sheets in Greenland and the entirety of Antarctica would melt. That would raise the global sea level by 200 feet.[1] When Statista published research on the effects of temperature levels rising by two degrees Celsius, it was estimated that more than 200 million people would be in danger of dying by 2100.[2] And that is just two degrees.

Despite the intensity of these last judgments, many people refuse to repent and even blaspheme God.

> **REVELATION 16:9**—"Men were scorched with great heat, and they blasphemed the name of God who has power over these plagues; and they did not repent and give Him glory."

In fact, Revelation describes people blaspheming God three times, and all three are listed in chapter 16 in verses 9, 11, and 21.

Ironically, the people curse God, who alone could solve their problems if they would only humble themselves and turn to Him. The people's lack of surrender is symptomatic of their stubborn hearts toward God and is another reminder that God's judgment is just.

Fifth Bowl

> **REVELATION 16:10-11**—"The fifth angel poured out his bowl on the throne of the beast, and his kingdom became full of darkness; and they gnawed their tongues because of the pain. They blasphemed the God of heaven because of their pains and their sores, and did not repent of their deeds."

During the fifth bowl judgment, darkness covers the kingdom of the beast. Some believe that this darkness covers only the area of Babylon—it depends on what is considered a part of the kingdom of the beast. This darkness is like a preview of hell, meant to encourage people to repent.

The sores that break out on people harken back to the first bowl judgment, indicating that the bowl judgments are coming in quick succession.

Sixth Bowl

The Euphrates River dries up.

> **REVELATION 16:12**–"The sixth angel poured out his bowl on the great river Euphrates, and its water was dried up, so that the way of the kings from the east might be prepared."

Then demons entice people to use the dried riverbed to foolishly wage war against God and His people Israel.

> **REVELATION 16:13-14**–"I saw three unclean spirits like frogs coming out of the mouth of the dragon, out of the mouth of the beast, and out of the mouth of the false prophet. For they are spirits of demons, performing signs, which go out to the kings of the earth and of the whole world, to gather them to the battle of that great day of God Almighty."

Armageddon

Then comes the battle of Armageddon.

> **REVELATION 16:15-16**–"'Behold, I am coming as a thief. Blessed is he who watches, and keeps his garments, lest he walk naked and they see his shame.' And they gathered them together to the place called in Hebrew, Armageddon."

Ezekiel 38–39 tells us that Russia, Turkey, Eastern Europe, and the northern African Islamic nations (Libya, Ethiopia, northern Sudan) will attack Israel at the *beginning* of the tribulation period and be wiped out.

Now, as we are nearing the end of the tribulation, demonic principalities incite the Middle and Far Eastern nations to cross the dried riverbed of the Euphrates and advance with military might against Israel. These would be the Islamic nations of Iraq, Iran, Afghanistan, and Pakistan, and likely their allies, India and China.

These nations will gather at the valley by Mount Megiddo to converge on Israel, and the battle will spill over all the way to the south by Jerusalem in the Kidron Valley.

"Megiddo" appears 12 times in the Old Testament and one time in the New Testament, where it is hidden in the name "Armageddon" (Revelation 16:16), a compound of *har,* meaning "hill," and *magedōn,* meaning "slaughter." Mount Megiddo will become literally "the hill of slaughter." Megiddo is in the Jezreel Valley, which is about 14 miles wide and about 24 miles long—a valley vast enough to host these enemy nations for the final, climactic battle of the tribulation period, which will be carried out against Israel.

But what starts at the hill of Megiddo ends in the Kidron Valley in Jerusalem.

The Kidron Valley is also known as the Valley of Jehoshaphat. The name *Jehoshaphat* means "God shall judge," so this valley's nickname literally translates to "the valley where Yahweh shall judge." That's an appropriate name, for it seems that though the nations will first gather at Megiddo, the Kidron Valley is where God will judge them.

Armageddon in the Old Testament

Zechariah the prophet sees this day coming.

> **Zechariah 14:1-4**—"Behold, the day of the Lord is coming, and your spoil will be divided in your midst. For I will gather all the nations to battle against Jerusalem; the city shall be taken, the houses rifled, and the women ravished. Half of the city shall go into captivity, but the remnant of the people shall not be cut off from the city.
>
> "Then the Lord will go forth and fight against those nations, as He fights in the day of battle. And in that day His feet will

> stand on the Mount of Olives, which faces Jerusalem on the east. And the Mount of Olives shall be split in two, from east to west, making a very large valley; half of the mountain shall move toward the north and half of it toward the south."

Ezekiel had a vision about the end, though there is debate as to whether he wrote about the battle of Armageddon itself, or about a series of battles that culminate with Armageddon. The latter is more likely.

> **Ezekiel 38:3-6**—"Thus says the Lord God: 'Behold, I am against you, O Gog, the prince of Rosh, Meshech, and Tubal. I will turn you around, put hooks into your jaws, and lead you out, with all your army, horses, and horsemen, all splendidly clothed, a great company with bucklers and shields, all of them handling swords. Persia, Ethiopia, and Libya are with them, all of them with shield and helmet; Gomer and all its troops; the house of Togarmah from the far north and all its troops—many people are with you.'"

"Gog" is a title that can be translated as "prince" or "czar," and in this case, "Gog" refers to the prince of Magog.

Historians Josephus, Pliny, and Herodotus thought "Magog" was the land of the ancient Scythians, those who lived north of the Black and the Caspian Seas—that is, Russia.

From the text, we can see Russia will take the lead in advancing against Israel, and the others listed will follow behind. We are seeing a coalition of countries form that the Bible predicted more than 2,500 years ago. These are the countries who will wage war against God's people:

1. Persia, which is modern-day Iran, used to be friendly with Israel, even exporting oil to them, till the Islamic Revolution of 1979 and a change of leadership made this country a staunch enemy of Israel. Today, Iran is an ally of Russia.
2. Ethiopia, which has a 34 percent Sunni Muslim population.[3]
3. Libya, which has a 97 percent Sunni Muslim population.[4] Libya represents the states in the upper-Nile region of Africa.

4. Gomer, which is the Eastern Europe region of Germany and Poland.
5. Togarmah, which is the region of Turkey, Armenia, and Georgia.

Ezekiel and Revelation Similarities

Both refer to how God will bring judgment on those who rise against Him. The wrath God pours out in Ezekiel 38 is similar to the judgment He brings with Him at the battle of Armageddon. Let us compare Ezekiel and Revelation:

1. They both speak of God's wrath

> **Ezekiel 38:18-19a**—"'It will come to pass at the same time, when Gog comes against the land of Israel,' says the Lord God, 'that My fury will show in My face. For in My jealousy and in the fire of My wrath I have spoken.'"

> **REVELATION 16:19**–"Now the great city was divided into three parts, and the cities of the nations fell. And great Babylon was remembered before God, to give her the cup of the wine of the fierceness of His wrath."

2. They both speak of a great earthquake

> **Ezekiel 38:19**—"In My jealousy and in the fire of My wrath I have spoken: 'Surely in that day there shall be a great earthquake in the land of Israel.'"

REVELATION 16:18–"There were noises and thunderings and lightnings; and there was a great earthquake, such a mighty and great earthquake as had not occurred since men were on the earth."

3. They both speak of the mountains

However, there is one difference; Ezekiel says the mountains will be thrown down, but Revelation says the mountains will not be found.

Ezekiel 38:20-21—"'The fish of the sea, the birds of the heavens, the beasts of the field, all creeping things that creep on the earth, and all men who are on the face of the earth shall shake at My presence. The mountains shall be thrown down, the steep places shall fall, and every wall shall fall to the ground. I will call for a sword against Gog throughout all My mountains,' says the Lord GOD. 'Every man's sword will be against his brother.'"

REVELATION 16:20–"Every island fled away, and the mountains were not found."

4. They both speak of pestilence, or plague

Ezekiel 38:22a—"I will bring him to judgment with pestilence and bloodshed."

REVELATION 16:21b–"Men blasphemed God because of the plague of the hail, since that plague was exceedingly great."

5. They both speak of great hailstones

> **Ezekiel 38:22b**—"I will rain down on him, on his troops, and on the many peoples who are with him, flooding rain, great hailstones, fire, and brimstone."

> **REVELATION 16:21a**–"Great hail from heaven fell upon men, each hailstone about the weight of a talent."

Some believe that these two passages do not refer to two distinct wars, but rather, to one long war that culminates in Armageddon. It appears that Ezekiel 38 speaks of Western armies, while Revelation 16 speaks of Eastern armies. Therefore, while the murmurs of war come from the Western armies at the beginning of the tribulation period, the Eastern armies join them by the end of the tribulation period, combining and culminating into the battle of Armageddon.

But whether there is peace in the time between Ezekiel 38 and Revelation 16, we do not know. What we can surmise is that what begins in Ezekiel ends in Revelation.

As a Thief

In Revelation 16, Jesus warned He will come as a thief.

> **REVELATION 16:15**–"Behold, I am coming as a thief. Blessed is he who watches, and keeps his garments, lest he walk naked and they see his shame."

But this is not the only time Jesus said He will come as a thief.

> **1 Thessalonians 5:2-4**—"You yourselves know perfectly that the day of the Lord so comes as a thief in the night. For when they say, 'Peace and safety!' then sudden destruction comes upon them, as labor pains upon a pregnant woman. And they

> shall not escape. But you, brethren, are not in darkness, so that this Day should overtake you as a thief."

Note how Jesus described the rapture and the second coming as a surprise, like one "coming as a thief." Events of the end times will be both surprising and sudden. Many people will be caught off guard, though believers should not be surprised. We should be ready!

> **2 Peter 3:10-12**—"The day of the Lord will come as a thief in the night, in which the heavens will pass away with a great noise, and the elements will melt with fervent heat; both the earth and the works that are in it will be burned up. Therefore, since all these things will be dissolved, what manner of persons ought you to be in holy conduct and godliness, looking for and hastening the coming of the day of God, because of which the heavens will be dissolved, being on fire, and the elements will melt with fervent heat?"

Seventh Bowl

> **REVELATION 16:17-19**–"The seventh angel poured out his bowl into the air, and a loud voice came out of the temple of heaven, from the throne, saying, 'It is done!' And there were noises and thunderings and lightnings; and there was a great earthquake, such a mighty and great earthquake as had not occurred since men were on the earth. Now the great city was divided into three parts, and the cities of the nations fell. And great Babylon was remembered before God, to give her the cup of the wine of the fierceness of His wrath."

For the seventh bowl, God also rains down hailstones weighing a talent (about 100 pounds) upon people. Then a severe earthquake splits the great city into three parts.

Some people speculate that the "great city" mentioned in verse 19 is Babylon, but I believe verse 19 speaks of Jerusalem because John was already briefing us about everything that is happening there.

In addition, the prophet Zechariah tells us that when Jesus returns to Earth, an earthquake will split the Mount of Olives, moving half of it to the north and half to the south (Zechariah 14:4). This splitting will result in a river of fresh water emerging from underneath the Temple Mount and meandering south through the new valley created by the splitting of the mountain (Zechariah 14:8). This river will end up in the Dead Sea, turning it into a freshwater source teeming with life (Ezekiel 47:9).

Men Blaspheming

Again, at the end of Revelation 16, men refuse to repent and instead, they blaspheme God. And God does not take pleasure in those who refuse to be saved. God is merciful, but there will still be many who refuse Him.

Reflections on Revelation 16

Getting Started

Revelation 16 covers the seven bowl judgments, which correspond to the golden bowls of incense in Revelation 15:7-8. What was the prayer of the martyrs (Revelation 6:9-10), and how do their prayers—represented by the incense bowls—lead to the judgments that rain on the earth (see Revelation 13:10; Revelation 16:5-6)?

Study Questions

1. What is the first bowl judgment (Revelation 16:1-2), and why were people complaining about the first bowl judgment during the fifth bowl judgment (Revelation 16:10-11)? How does this display the character of God (see Exodus 9:1-4, 10-12; Proverbs 30:5; 2 Peter 2:9)?
2. What happens in the second and third bowl judgments (Revelation 16:3-4), and how do the methods of judgment paint a picture of the people's sins, and the specific evils they have committed (see Revelation 16:5-7)?
3. What are the effects of the second and third bowl judgments (Revelation 16:3-4)? How are these secondary effects meant to lead people to God (see Psalms 38:14-15; 39:4-7; Isaiah 40:8)?
4. What is the fourth bowl judgment (Revelation 16:8), and how does this judgment affect Earth's geology?
5. What is the fifth bowl judgment (Revelation 16:10-11), and how do the fourth and fifth bowl judgments work together to warn unbelievers and call them to repentance (see Matthew 8:10-12; 25:41; Mark 9:47-48)?
6. What is the sixth bowl judgment (Revelation 16:12), and

how does this judgment pave the way for the battle of Armageddon (Revelation 16:13-16)?

7. Armageddon will start at Megiddo and end at Kidron Valley (Revelation 16:15-16). What is significant about the names of these locations, and what do they tell us about God (see Ecclesiastes 3:17; Romans 2:1-6)?
8. What similarities do we find between the battles in Ezekiel 38:18-22 and Revelation 16:18-21? And how do we reconcile the different locations of the armies (see Ezekiel 38:3-6; Revelation 16:12)?
9. What does God's ability to predict the coming enmity between Iran (then called Persia) and Israel in Ezekiel 38:5 tell us about God (see Psalms 139:4; 147:5; Isaiah 46:9-10)?
10. What happens during the seventh bowl judgment (Revelation 16:17-19), and how does this judgment demonstrate God's sovereign hand?

Important Takeaways for Us Today

1. How do people react to God's wrath in Revelation 16:9, 11, and 21? What is ironic about the way unbelievers react to receiving God's just judgment (see Ezekiel 33:11), and what principle can we take away from this about how to react when we face God's chastisement (see Hebrews 12:5-11; Revelation 3:19)?
2. In Revelation 16:15, why is Jesus' coming compared to that of a thief in the night (see 1 Thessalonians 5:2-4; 2 Peter 3:10-12)? How should this change the way we live (see Matthew 24:42-44; Revelation 22:12)?

17

The Fall of the One-World Religion

REVELATION 17

If you recall, in Revelation 12, we discussed a woman who symbolized God's people Israel, but that is not the same woman as the one riding the beast in Revelation 17. This woman, rather than being persecuted by the dragon, will ride the dragon to prominence, gaining dominance over the nations of the earth. But Jesus is Judge, and He will bring wrath against spiritual Babylon, making her fall faster than she arose.

Context

Babylon

Chapters 17 and 18 are both about Babylon, but chapter 17 discusses the *spiritual* component, while chapter 18 discusses the *commercial* component. However, both commercial and spiritual Babylon will have their headquarters in the same location.

Some believe John wrote about a figurative Babylon, but I believe the Babylon in Iraq will be literally rebuilt and destroyed.

Scriptural Mentions

Babylon is no stranger to Scripture. The Bible mentions this place more times than any other city except Jerusalem. In fact, Babylon is referred to 300 times. In Revelation alone, 42 of the book's 404 verses refer to Babylon by name or inference. That is about one out of every ten verses in Revelation. God has a lot to say about Babylon!

Geography

Babylon is about 55 miles south of Baghdad, along the Euphrates River in Iraq. In its glory days under Nebuchadnezzar, the Hanging Gardens of Babylon were considered one of the seven wonders of the ancient world.

Architecture

Babylon was once known for its strength and power. Historians tell us that Babylon's walls were exceptionally high and thick. The Babylonians also diverted the Euphrates River through and around the city to form a moat as an extra layer of defense.

This is a major reason why Babylon was considered impenetrable.

Isaiah's Prophecy

God predicted Babylon's downfall. In Isaiah chapters 47–49, 150 years before the fall of Babylon, God not only said that the Babylonian Empire would fall, but also that King Cyrus of Persia would bring it down to replace the empire with his own.

Cyrus's Victory

Cyrus saw that the Babylonians had diverted the Euphrates under their city walls to be a source of fresh water, so he stopped up the Euphrates a few miles upstream and used the dry riverbed to walk under the city walls and subdue Babylon. Thus, the impenetrable city fell on October 12, 539 BC.

Rebuilding Attempts

Saddam Hussein tried to rebuild Babylon during the 1980s when he ruled Iraq, even having a coin made with his face on one side and Nebuchadnezzar's face on the other. Hussein built one of his palaces on the old foundation of Nebuchadnezzar's palace. During this time, Hussein also attempted to annex Kuwait. For this attempt, he had sanctions placed on him. And when war broke out, he was captured, tried, and hanged. His efforts failed, but eventually, someone will rebuild the city. Right now, Babylon lies in ruins, but one day, this city will be the commercial and spiritual center of the world until God destroys it.

The Woman

The woman is not a literal woman, but a picture. She is called a prostitute in the NIV and ESV Bibles, and a harlot in verses 1, 15, and 16 of the NKJV Bible.

And in verse 5, we see her title:

> **REVELATION 17:5**—"On her forehead a name was written: MYSTERY, BABYLON THE GREAT, THE MOTHER OF HARLOTS AND OF THE ABOMINATIONS OF THE EARTH."

This woman represents a false world religion that rises on the back of the Antichrist.

How the Woman Comes to Be

The Bible records a tale of two cities: Jerusalem as the city of peace, and Babylon as the city of confusion. And the woman represents the second city: Babylon.

Babylon had its beginnings in Genesis and was founded by Nimrod, who began conquering the world after the flood.

> **Genesis 10:8-12**—"Cush begot Nimrod; he began to be a mighty one on the earth. He was a mighty hunter before the LORD; therefore it is said, 'Like Nimrod the mighty hunter before the LORD.' And the beginning of his kingdom was Babel, Erech, Accad, and Calneh, in the land of Shinar. From that land he went to Assyria and built Nineveh, Rehoboth Ir, Calah, and Resen between Nineveh and Calah (that is the principal city)."

Tower of Babel

"Babel" is an ancient name for Babylon, and "Shinar" is the ancient name for Mesopotamia or Babylonia. The founder of both was Nimrod, the "mighty hunter before the LORD." This title sounds nice, but do not be fooled. "Nimrod" means "rebellious one," or "rebellion." And his title as a hunter "before the Lord" translates in Hebrew as *pānîm*, meaning "face." So, this turn of phrase means "one who got in God's face."

This was the man who made Babel one of his building projects. It was under his direction that men made the Tower of Babel (Genesis 11), which was a ziggurat, a pyramid with a staircase on the exterior that led to an overlook at the pinnacle. The Greek historian Herodotus recorded seeing a ziggurat that was 700 feet high. By comparison, the Washington Monument is only 555 feet high.[1] Imagine how enormous the tower was!

At the time, everyone spoke one language, yet they used their unity to oppose God, to worship the stars, and to make a name for themselves. From this same Babel came all witchcraft, so God decided to confound the people by making them speak different languages, which caused them to scatter.

Birthplace of Idols

Semiramis, wife of Nimrod, was considered the queen of heaven. Tammuz was their son. Legend stated that Tammuz was conceived in a miraculous way, was gored by a boar, and rose from the dead.

The legend took root, and in Babel, the people began worshipping the mother-son duo of Semiramis and Tammuz. The Assyrians worshipped Ishtar and Tammuz, the Canaanites worshipped Ashtoreth and Baal, the Egyptians worshipped Isis and Horus, the Greeks worshipped Aphrodite and Eros, and the Romans worshipped Venus and Cupid. These are all cultic mother-son combinations that began in Babylon. Even as recently as the 1980s, Iraq named its nuclear reactor Tammuz. In a secret military operation in 1981, Israel dispatched F-15s and F-16s that flew at low altitudes to Iraq and destroyed the reactor.

We shouldn't be surprised that the birthplace of false religion will rise again from the ashes of Babylon, until Jesus brings this place to permanent ruin.

One-World Religion

The rapture will remove all Christians from Earth, and eventually, the number of tribulation converts will be many (Revelation 7:9). Some speculate that the vacuum will be filled with an amalgamation of various religions. Even now, some say that people of different religious backgrounds all worship the same God and that all paths lead to God. Be wary of this ecumenical movement—not all who claim to belong to God truly do.

Others believe that because Islam is already a prominent faith, it will become the one-world religion. Either way, the faith of the end times will be a false religion spearheaded by the False Prophet, who will lead people away from God and toward the Antichrist.

The Woman and the Beast

Many Waters

> **REVELATION 17:1**–"One of the seven angels who had the seven bowls came and talked with me, saying to me, 'Come, I will show you the judgment of the great harlot who sits on many waters.'"

This woman, spiritual Babylon, will sit on "many waters." Verse 15 clarifies that this is figuratively speaking of this false religion's global influence.

> **REVELATION 17:15**–"He said to me, 'The waters which you saw, where the harlot sits, are peoples, multitudes, nations, and tongues.'"

Her Fornication

> **REVELATION 17:2**–"...with whom the kings of the earth committed fornication, and the inhabitants of the earth were made drunk with the wine of her fornication."

"Fornication" here signifies spiritual adultery; that is, holding allegiance to any other but the one true God, which is true of all false religions.

On a Scarlet Beast

> **REVELATION 17:3**–"He carried me away in the Spirit into the wilderness. And I saw a woman sitting on a scarlet beast which was full of names of blasphemy, having seven heads and ten horns."

This means that the woman and the False Prophet will ride to prominence at the same time as the beast, the Antichrist.

Purple and Scarlet

> **REVELATION 17:4-5**–"The woman was arrayed in purple and scarlet, and adorned with gold and precious stones and pearls, having in her hand a golden cup full of abominations and the filthiness of her fornication. And on her forehead a name was written:
>
> "MYSTERY, BABYLON THE GREAT, THE MOTHER OF HARLOTS AND OF THE ABOMINATIONS OF THE EARTH."

The purple and scarlet suggest that spiritual Babylon will be associated with wealth and nobility, and the gemstones symbolize the financial power this religion will hold. Because of these ties to opulence, some speculate that John was referring to the Roman Catholic Church and suggest that the pope will be the Antichrist. But the religion described in Revelation 17 suggests something much larger than Catholicism.

Besides this, despite some unbiblical tenets held by the Roman Catholic Church, not all Catholics are unsaved. There are a small number of Catholics who understand that salvation is through Christ alone, by grace alone, yet still attend Catholic churches.

Martyrs of Jesus

> **REVELATION 17:6**–"I saw the woman, drunk with the blood of the saints and with the blood of the martyrs of Jesus. And when I saw her, I marveled with great amazement."

The woman's drunken state tells us that the world religion will be promoted through violence against believers. Some believe this could be the advancing of Islam by the sword.

The Meaning of the Woman and the Beast

Seven Kings

> **REVELATION 17:7-9**–"The angel said to me, 'Why did you marvel? I will tell you the mystery of the woman and of the beast that carries her, which has the seven heads and the ten horns. The beast that you saw was, and is not, and will ascend out of the bottomless pit and go to perdition. And those who dwell on the earth will marvel, whose names are not written in the Book of Life from the foundation of the world, when they see the beast that was, and is not, and yet is.
>
> "Here is the mind which has wisdom: The seven heads are seven mountains on which the woman sits.'"

The seven heads, or the seven mountains, are the "seven kings" referenced in verse 10. Hence, when John says "the woman sits" on the seven, he was saying that the woman, who represents the coming global religion, will sit in a place of political power over them.

The seven kings she will sit on are also figurative, representing seven global empires.

> **REVELATION 17:10**–"There are also seven kings. Five have fallen, one is, and the other has not yet come. And when he comes, he must continue a short time."

The phrase "five have fallen" is in the past tense. This refers to the five world-dominating empires that have come before John: the Egyptian, Assyrian, Babylonian, Medo-Persian, and Greek empires.

The phrase "one is" speaks of the present empire from John's perspective, the Roman Empire.

And the phrase "the other has not yet come" is in the future tense, for the seventh global empire will be led by the Antichrist.

Confederation of Nations

> **REVELATION 17:11**—"The beast that was, and is not, is himself also the eighth, and is of the seven, and is going to perdition."

The beast is "the eighth" but "of the seven." This means that the seven kings referenced in verse 10 will form the confederation of nations, of which the Antichrist will take part. But the Antichrist will come out of that to become a world dictator.

This confederation will be made up of ten kings:

> **REVELATION 17:12**—"The ten horns which you saw are ten kings who have received no kingdom as yet, but they receive authority for one hour as kings with the beast."

Remember, the "horn" here is a symbol of authority and power, and the ten kings, or horns, will make up the confederation of nations. This government will consist of ten regions represented by ten kings united into one system. When we look at the European Union, we can see how there are geographical regions in which people come together under common law. The prospect of this happening seems less far-fetched now than before.

But this system will last for only "one hour."

> **REVELATION 17:13**—"These are of one mind, and they will give their power and authority to the beast."

We do not know whether the Antichrist will persuade them or Satan will beguile them, but the ten kings will hand their authority over to the beast. Of course, the Antichrist will make war with the Lamb, Jesus Christ, and eventually be defeated.

> **REVELATION 17:14**—"These will make war with the Lamb, and the Lamb will overcome them, for He is Lord of lords and King of kings; and those who are with Him are called, chosen, and faithful."

But until then, the Antichrist will rule over the nations with the support of the harlot, the false religion spearheaded by the False Prophet. Ironically, the ten kings will come to hate the harlot even though it was through their allowance that she gained such prominence.

> **REVELATION 17:16-18**—"The ten horns which you saw on the beast, these will hate the harlot, make her desolate and naked, eat her flesh and burn her with fire. For God has put it into their hearts to fulfill His purpose, to be of one mind, and to give their kingdom to the beast, until the words of God are fulfilled. And the woman whom you saw is that great city which reigns over the kings of the earth."

Ultimately, the ten kings will destroy the world religion and give all the power to the Antichrist, whom they will worship.

Reflections on Revelation 17

Getting Started

Throughout chapter 17, John described the ugly plan of the enemy to blaspheme God and oppose His saints (Revelation 17:4-6), but we know that God uses evil to accomplish His purposes (Revelation 17:16-17) for a time. What does this tell us about the way God's sovereignty and man's free will operate in our world (see Exodus 8:15; 10:20, 27; Psalm 76:10; Matthew 26:24)?

Study Questions

1. What two cities does Scripture mention the most, and how do they contrast each other (see 1 Chronicles 23:25; 2 Chronicles 6:6; Revelation 17:5; 18:2)?
2. What does Isaiah's prophecy regarding the fall of ancient Babylon tell us about God (see Job 12:23; Psalms 22:28; 46:5-6)?
3. In Revelation 17, what does the prostitute woman represent (Revelation 17:5)? How does her nature (Revelation 17:1-5) differ from how she presents herself (See Revelation 17:4)? What does this contrast warn against (see Matthew 7:15; 23:27-28)?
4. How does Babylon's founder (see Genesis 10:8-12) compare with Israel's founder, Abraham (Genesis 15:3-6; 18:17-19; Hebrews 11:8, 17)? What makes us children of Abraham (see Galatians 3:7-9)?
5. For what purpose will a one-world religion be created? How does the purpose and unity of this religion parallel that of the people building the Tower of Babel (see Genesis 11:1, 6-9)?
6. What kinds of power does the prostitute wield (Revelation

17:4-9)? How is her downfall a warning against using power for evil (see Psalm 94:1-15)?

7. What do the seven kings and ten horns symbolize (Revelation 17:10-12)? How do they herald in the world religion and the Antichrist (Revelation 17:7-9, 13)?
8. When the kings discard the prostitute, who do they replace her with (Revelation 17:13, 16-18)?
9. When the nations unite to war against God and His people, the Lord overcomes them (Revelation 17:14). How do the names of God used in verse 14 affirm Christ's victory (see Psalm 93:1-2; Romans 5:9; 1 Corinthians 8:6; Hebrews 10:11-14)?
10. In Revelation 17:14, how does God describe His people? What do these titles tell us about how God sees us (see Matthew 25:21; 1 Peter 2:9)? How should our identity in Christ change us (see John 15:16)?

Important Takeaways for Us Today

1. Just as the false religion of Revelation 17 will have a corrupting effect on the nations (see Revelation 17:1-2, 15), we as God's people are to have a preservative effect on the nations (see Matthew 5:14-15; Luke 14:34). What are some ways we can be salt and light to others (see Matthew 5:16; 10:27; 2 Corinthians 4:5-6; Colossians 4:6)?
2. Though the prostitute wields political, economic, military, and religious power, she still ends up destroyed. What should we learn from her fall from power (see Psalms 2:1-5; 20:7; 60:11; Proverbs 11:28)?

18

The Fall of the One-World Government

REVELATION 18

Would you believe someone who tells you that America will fall in a day? This would sound crazy because America has stood strong through world wars and a great depression. Yet Babylon will face God's judgment in one day and fall, "for strong is the Lord God who judges her" (Revelation 18:8). And there are two different reactions to her fall: the mourning of the worldly and the rejoicing of the saints.

Babylon Falls

Another Angel

> **REVELATION 18:1**—"After these things I saw another angel coming down from heaven, having great authority, and the earth was illuminated with his glory."

Some think this angel is Jesus, but this angel is described as "another," *allos* in the Greek text, meaning "another of the same kind." That is, another of the same kind of angel as appeared in chapter 17.

Therefore, this angelic being possesses the glory given to angels, not the glory belonging to God alone.

Babylon Has Fallen

> **REVELATION 18:2**—"He cried mightily with a loud voice, saying, 'Babylon the great is fallen, is fallen, and has become a dwelling place of demons, a prison for every foul spirit, and a cage for every unclean and hated bird!'"

The fall of Babylon is repeated for emphasis. This will be the day of destruction for the Babylonian world system.

Wine of Fornication

> **REVELATION 18:3**—"All the nations have drunk of the wine of the wrath of her fornication, the kings of the earth have committed fornication with her, and the merchants of the earth have become rich through the abundance of her luxury."

Nations will become intoxicated with materialism and greed because of Babylon, the trophy of commercialism and trade. If we pay attention, we will find that this level of greed is not far-fetched, for there is covetousness inside every human heart.

This does not mean that God has something against material things or wealth. Rather, this means that not everyone can handle wealth wisely. Lottery winners often find themselves becoming addicted to drugs, depressed, or even dead because they fail to exercise proper stewardship of their newfound wealth.

God gives man the ability to produce wealth, and He gives His people guidelines as to how to use the resources entrusted to us.

Deuteronomy 8:18—"You shall remember the Lord your God, for it is He who gives you power to get wealth, that He may establish His covenant which He swore to your fathers, as it is this day."

Biblical Stewardship

God wants us to remember that our identity is in Him and not the stuff money can buy. Instead, whether we have little or much, we must be good stewards of what He has entrusted to us. That means we must live within our means and be generous with what we have.

God wants us to be at peace with what He has given us—to be content rather than greedy.

Challenging Statistics[1]

The worldly system of materialism and greed does not come out of nowhere. Babylon is not just something far ahead. In some ways, Babylon is already here:

1. There are 300,000 items in the average American home.
2. The average American home has tripled in size over the last 50 years.
3. Off-site storage has been the fastest-growing segment of the commercial real-estate industry over the last four decades, and one out of every ten Americans rent storage space.
4. Twenty-five percent of people with two-car garages do not have room to park cars inside them due to their extra possessions, and 32 percent have room for only one vehicle.
5. The United States has upward of 50,000 storage facilities—more than five times the number of Starbucks.
6. Currently, there is 7.3 square feet of self-storage space for every man, woman, and child in America; thus, it is physically possible that every American could simultaneously stand atop the total canopy of self-storage roofing.

7. Only 3.1 percent of the world's children live in America, but they own 40 percent of the toys consumed globally.
8. The average American woman owns 30 outfits—that is one for every day of the month. In 1930, they owned nine.
9. The average American throws away 65 pounds of clothing per year.
10. Americans spend more on shoes, clothing, watches—$100 billion—than on higher education.

Come Out

> **REVELATION 18:4**–"I heard another voice from heaven saying, 'Come out of her, my people, lest you share in her sins, and lest you receive of her plagues.'"

God calls His people to separate themselves from the world's greedy economic systems. Again, Christians will be raptured before the start of the tribulation, but some will become believers afterward, and those are the people to whom God speaks here.

We are to be set apart unto the Lord, to be in the world but not of the world—a common theme in the Bible.

Babylon Judged

> **REVELATION 18:5-7**–"Her sins have reached to heaven, and God has remembered her iniquities. Render to her just as she rendered to you, and repay her double according to her works; in the cup which she has mixed, mix double for her. In the measure that she glorified herself and lived luxuriously, in the same measure give her torment and sorrow; for she says in her heart, 'I sit as queen, and am no widow, and will not see sorrow.'"

The Judge of all the earth will not leave Babylon unpunished. And when God judges Babylon, He will give her swift destruction.

> **REVELATION 18:8**–"Therefore her plagues will come in one day—death and mourning and famine. And she will be utterly burned with fire, for strong is the Lord God who judges her."

Again, this seems to be a literal Babylon, for John spoke of a city burned by fire. If Babylon were simply a figurative representation of a world economic system, the city would not need to be burned down.

Earth Mourns

> **REVELATION 18:9-11**–"The kings of the earth who committed fornication and lived luxuriously with her will weep and lament for her, when they see the smoke of her burning, standing at a distance for fear of her torment, saying, 'Alas, alas, that great city Babylon, that mighty city! For in one hour your judgment has come.'
>
> "And the merchants of the earth will weep and mourn over her, for no one buys their merchandise anymore."

John described a domino effect that follows the burning of Babylon, and then gave a list of commodities and assets that will be destroyed alongside the fall of the global economic system.

> **REVELATION 18:12-14**–"Merchandise of gold and silver, precious stones and pearls, fine linen and purple, silk and scarlet, every kind of citron wood, every kind of object of ivory, every kind of object of most precious wood, bronze, iron, and marble; and cinnamon and incense, fragrant oil and frankincense, wine and oil, fine flour and wheat, cattle and sheep, horses

> and chariots, and bodies and souls of men. The fruit that your soul longed for has gone from you, and all the things which are rich and splendid have gone from you, and you shall find them no more at all."

John described an economic catastrophe of unparalleled proportions. Talk about a stock market crash!

> **REVELATION 18:15-17**–"The merchants of these things, who became rich by her, will stand at a distance for fear of her torment, weeping and wailing, and saying, 'Alas, alas, that great city that was clothed in fine linen, purple, and scarlet, and adorned with gold and precious stones and pearls! For in one hour such great riches came to nothing.' Every shipmaster, all who travel by ship, sailors, and as many as trade on the sea, stood at a distance."

"Shipmaster" is translated as "captain" in some Bibles, and these people will be as upset about the fall of their wealth as the kings and merchants.

> **REVELATION 18:18-19**–"[They] cried out when they saw the smoke of her burning, saying, 'What is like this great city?'
>
> "They threw dust on their heads and cried out, weeping and wailing, and saying, 'Alas, alas, that great city, in which all who had ships on the sea became rich by her wealth! For in one hour she is made desolate.'"

Between all these different verses, we see that kings, merchants, and sailors will weep and lament their material loss but not their spiritual loss. Sadly, this economic collapse will not bring them to the realization of the importance of God over these temporary things.

Also, we see in these verses that God knocks down every idol. Perhaps you have noticed in your own life the same principle, that God will work to remove what you have grown to prioritize over Him.

Heaven Rejoices

God tells His people to rejoice at Babylon's destruction, for He has avenged them.

> **REVELATION 18:20**–"Rejoice over her, O heaven, and you holy apostles and prophets, for God has avenged you on her!"

What a contrast this is to the way the world is mourning the downfall of their material wealth.

Not Found Anymore

> **REVELATION 18:21**–"Then a mighty angel took up a stone like a great millstone and threw it into the sea, saying, 'Thus with violence the great city Babylon shall be thrown down, and shall not be found anymore.'"

God will destroy both the corrupt city and the global economic system.

> **REVELATION 18:22-24**–"The sound of harpists, musicians, flutists, and trumpeters shall not be heard in you anymore. No craftsman of any craft shall be found in you anymore, and the sound of a millstone shall not be heard in you anymore. The light of a lamp shall not shine in you anymore, and the voice of bridegroom and bride shall not be heard in you anymore. For your merchants were the great men of the earth, for by your sorcery all the nations were deceived. And in her was found the blood of prophets and saints, and of all that were slain upon the earth."

And thus, God brings an end to spiritual Babylon in chapter 17 and to economic Babylon in chapter 18, as Paul prophesied.

> **2 Thessalonians 2:8**—"Then the lawless one will be revealed, whom the Lord will consume with the breath of His mouth and destroy with the brightness of His coming."

Reflections on Revelation 18

Getting Started

What is the difference between Babylon's fall in chapter 17 and Babylon's fall in chapter 18? What does God's quick victory over both powers (see 2 Thessalonians 2:8; Revelation 17:16-18; 18:21) emphasize about who He is (see Exodus 15:11; Psalm 50:1; Isaiah 9:6; Jeremiah 32:17)?

Study Questions

1. What kind of glory does the angel in Revelation 18:1 possess? What does it mean that God's creation possesses a form of glory (see Psalm 19:1; 1 Corinthians 15:38-41), and how do we cultivate that kind of glory (see Psalm 108:1; Proverbs 4:7-9; 19:11)?
2. What are the merchants intoxicated with (Revelation 18:3), and how do you see this same intoxication present in our culture (see Matthew 6:19-21, 24; Luke 12:15; 1 Timothy 6:6-10, 17-19; Hebrews 13:5)?
3. Instead of becoming drunk with the riches of this world, we are called to acknowledge the God who gave us the ability to gain resources (see Deuteronomy 8:18). How can you regularly acknowledge God's provision (see 1 Chronicles 29:14; Proverbs 3:5-6; Haggai 2:6-8; 1 Corinthians 10:31; James 1:17)?
4. What does the Bible say about how God expects us to steward our resources, and how do we put this principle in action (see Proverbs 13:22; 19:17; Matthew 6:33; 2 Corinthians 9:7; Philippians 4:10-19; 1 Timothy 5:8)?
5. In many ways, Babylon is already here (Revelation 18:3). Review the challenging statistics regarding American materialism and consider how you and your family can stand

for contentment in Christ amid this culture (see Proverbs 16:8; Isaiah 26:3; Acts 20:35; Galatians 6:14; Philippians 2:3).

6. What does God's call for His people to come out of Babylon (Revelation 18:4) convey about His heart toward us (see John 15:19; 17:1, 6, 9-17; 2 Corinthians 11:2; Romans 12:2)?
7. How does God judge Babylon (Revelation 18:4-8), and how do these judgments correspond to her sins (see Matthew 23:12; Luke 12:15-21)?
8. Revelation 18:12-19 records the merchants, kings, and sailors mourning Babylon's fall and their wealth with her, but what are they tragically failing to mourn? What does God want us to be rich in (see Romans 13:14; 1 Timothy 6:18; 1 Peter 1:6-7; Revelation 3:16-19)?
9. God will cause the wealthy to lose the material goods they worshipped (Revelation 18:18-19). What are some modern idols that you have fallen into (see Matthew 6:24; Colossians 3:4-5), and how has God used circumstances to pull you away from these idols (see Psalms 94:12; 118:18; 119:67, 71)?
10. What can we learn from heaven rejoicing over Babylon's destruction in Revelation 18:20 (see Proverbs 21:15; Romans 1:20)?

Important Takeaways for Us Today

1. Revelation 18:21 describes how Babylon will "not be found anymore." How does this exemplify the difference between the impermanence of man and the permanence of God (see Psalms 90:2; 119:89-90; Ecclesiastes 1:11; 3:1-3; 5:15; Hebrews 13:8)?
2. How should we conduct ourselves knowing that worldly systems will fade away (see Colossians 2:1-2; 2 Peter 3:10-14; 1 John 2:15-17)?

19

The Conquering King

REVELATION 19

Imagine you are at the wedding of a dear friend, and people are eating, laughing, and enjoying themselves, when a stranger tries to sneak into the party looking like they had just played a muddy game of football. Would you be appalled? Would you think, *How could someone come in, not even having any relationship with the happy couple, and not being properly dressed for the occasion?* It is the same with the marriage supper of our Lord. We must know the Groom and be dressed in His righteousness to enter and be blessed with "those who are called to the marriage supper of the Lamb!" (Revelation 19:9). Otherwise, you will fall before Him ashamed. Are you ready?

Context

Jesus' Second Coming

The first part of Christ's second coming is when He will come meet us in the air to take the church from the earth; we call this the rapture. And the second part is when He will come to Earth to rescue Israel and to establish the millennial kingdom.

Sights and Sounds

Revelation 19 comes in two parts: The first part records the events John heard in heaven, and the second part includes the sights John described.

Hence, verses 1 and 6 use the phrase "I heard," while verses 11, 17, and 19 use the phrase "I saw."

Rejoicing in Heaven

Hallelujah

> **REVELATION 19:1**—"After these things I heard a loud voice of a great multitude in heaven, saying, 'Alleluia! Salvation and glory and honor and power belong to the Lord our God!'"

The phrase "after these things," *meta tauta* in the Greek text, references the end of Babylon as reported in Revelation 17–18. This causes heaven's residents to rejoice, saying "Alleluia," a word of praise repeated four times in the first ten verses. These are also the only four times this word appears in Revelation.

Some translations use "hallelujah" rather than "alleluia," but they are the same word.

"Alleluia" is the Greek transliteration of the Hebrew *hallēlouia*, while "hallelujah" is a combination of two words: *hallel*, meaning "to praise, or to worship," and *Yah*, meaning "Yahweh," the name of God. Put together, "hallelujah" means "to praise Yahweh."

The original Greek manuscripts have the article "the" before every noun of verse 1. This means verse 1 should read: "Alleluia! *The* salvation, and *the* glory, and *the* honor, and *the* power belong to *the* Lord our God!" (emphasis added). This stresses that God is the only path to salvation, and the great virtues of God are sourced in God alone.

God's Judgments

> **REVELATION 19:2a**–"True and righteous are His judgments, because He has judged the great harlot who corrupted the earth with her fornication."

The time of God's true and righteous judgment does come. Though we may become confused and frustrated by the way those who are evil thrive, we must remember that God will deal with them in His time.

But sometimes we struggle with the fact evil is prospering and imagine God's judgment is delayed. The writer of Psalm 73 also wrestled with the abundance of evil on the earth and wondered where God was, but in the end, he sought God and gained an eternal perspective.

> **Psalm 73:16-17**—"When I thought how to understand this, it was too painful for me—until I went into the sanctuary of God; then I understood their end."

And part of God's justice includes Him avenging His people.

> **REVELATION 19:2b**–"He has avenged on her the blood of His servants shed by her."

As we read in the earlier chapters of Revelation, the saints will be martyred, but God will keep His promise to avenge them.

> **Revelation 6:9-10**—"When He opened the fifth seal, I saw under the altar the souls of those who had been slain for the word of God and for the testimony which they held. And they cried with a loud voice, saying, 'How long, O Lord, holy and true, until You judge and avenge our blood on those who dwell on the earth?'"

Forever and Ever

> **REVELATION 19:3**—"Again they said, 'Alleluia! Her smoke rises up forever and ever!'"

The saints will rejoice in God's justice that will permanently bring down the evil systems of this world. Among those worshipping in heaven will be the 24 elders who represent the raptured church, and the four living creatures who are the angelic beings that attend to God around the throne:

> **REVELATION 19:4**—"The twenty-four elders and the four living creatures fell down and worshiped God who sat on the throne, saying, 'Amen! Alleluia!'"

Marriage of the Lamb

> **REVELATION 19:5-7**—"A voice came from the throne, saying, 'Praise our God, all you His servants and those who fear Him, both small and great!'
>
> "And I heard, as it were, the voice of a great multitude, as the sound of many waters and as the sound of mighty thunderings, saying, 'Alleluia! For the Lord God Omnipotent reigns! Let us be glad and rejoice and give Him glory, for the marriage of the Lamb has come, and His wife has made herself ready.'"

This passage compares the marriage of the Lamb to a Jewish wedding, which included the betrothal, the return of the groom, and the banquet.

Earthly Marriage

Before we can look at the symbolism implied in "the marriage of the Lamb," we must look at what the Hebrew marriage customs were in the first century AD.

Betrothal

The betrothal period was a time during which the fathers of the bride and groom would agree to a contract between the spouses-to-be. These arrangements could be made for children who were as young as two years old, and the children would marry when they were of a marriageable age.

The father of the groom would pay a dowry to the father of the bride, and this bride price could serve as alimony in case of a divorce because it was difficult in those days for a woman to support herself without a husband.

There was no marriage celebration or consummation during a betrothal, but rather, the groom left for one year to build an addition to his father's house. Three to four generations of a family would typically live together in the same home. The betrothed groom was also exempt from military duty during this time.

Though the man and woman did not have sexual intimacy at this point, they were considered married and could dissolve that agreement only through divorce. Remember, Joseph was about to quietly divorce the virgin Mary when he thought she had been unfaithful (Matthew 1:19).

Return

At the end of the betrothal period, the groom would return for his bride.

Matthew 25 illustrates this with the parable of the ten virgins, or bridesmaids, showing that not everyone will be ready for Jesus' return. The five who try to borrow oil when the groom arrives are turned away because you cannot get to God on borrowed faith.

Banquet

When the groom returned for the bride, the wedding party would hoist the bride up on their shoulders and to her father-in-law's house for a seven-day feast. The banquet was when the bride and groom consummated the marriage.

In Scripture, we get a glimpse of what marriage banquets were like. John 2 records that Jesus' first miracle on Earth, turning water to wine, happened at a wedding banquet in Cana.

Heavenly Marriage

But how do Jewish first-century marriage customs relate to Jesus' return?

Betrothal

Jesus paid the bride price for us with His blood, and He enters a covenant with us who accept His offer of salvation. During this time, Jesus is preparing a place for us in heaven.

> **John 14:2**—"In My Father's house are many mansions; if it were not so, I would have told you. I go to prepare a place for you."

We are currently in the betrothal period with Christ.

Return

We are to be looking for and anticipating the return of the Bridegroom because one day He will return, and we must be ready.

> **John 14:3**—"If I go and prepare a place for you, I will come again and receive you to Myself; that where I am, there you may be also."

Banquet

This is what Revelation 19 describes: the day when we are finally with the Lord.

Bride and Groom

The bride is a picture of the church. In Scripture she is called the bride of Christ, and she will be clothed in the purity of God.

> **REVELATION 19:8-9**—"To her it was granted to be arrayed in fine linen, clean and bright, for the fine linen is the righteous acts of the saints.
>
> "Then he said to me, 'Write: "Blessed are those who are called to the marriage supper of the Lamb!"' And he said to me, 'These are the true sayings of God.'"

In biblical typology, or language, the New Testament church is the bride and Jesus is the Bridegroom. In fact, Paul uses the same sort of language in his letter to the Corinthians:

> **2 Corinthians 11:2**—"I am jealous for you with godly jealousy. For I have betrothed you to one husband, that I may present you as a chaste virgin to Christ."

The Bridegroom is Jesus, and He described Himself by His redemptive title many times in Revelation. In this book, "the Lamb" is His most-used title.

This is the way Jesus emphasized the bride price He paid for us, His bride.

Fellow Servant

> **REVELATION 19:10**—"I fell at his feet to worship him. But he said to me, 'See that you do not do that! I am your fellow servant, and of your brethren who have the testimony of Jesus. Worship God! For the testimony of Jesus is the spirit of prophecy.'"

John was so overwhelmed by the sights he saw that he fell to worship the angel, but the angel rightly corrected him, for only God deserves our worship.

Jesus Returns as Judge

Jesus Returns

> **REVELATION 19:11**–"Now I saw heaven opened, and behold, a white horse. And He who sat on him was called Faithful and True, and in righteousness He judges and makes war."

During His first coming, Jesus rode on a donkey, meek and mild. But in His second coming, He will ride on a white horse, waging war and bringing victory. He will come with the title "Faithful and True"—that is our Lord! And He will come to bring justice.

Diadēma

> **REVELATION 19:12**–"His eyes were like a flame of fire, and on His head were many crowns. He had a name written that no one knew except Himself."

John described Jesus' eyes like fire to show that He will come to judge the Antichrist and those with him. While the Antichrist will come with a perishable laurel crown, *stephanos*, Jesus will come after him with imperishable royal crowns, *diadēma*. The temporary rule of the Antichrist will fade away before the coming of the King of kings.

Word of God

> **REVELATION 19:13**–"He was clothed with a robe dipped in blood, and His name is called The Word of God."

The Greek term for "word" is *logos*, meaning "expression" or "speech." But in that day, Greek philosophy used *logos* to mean "divine revelation." Thus, Jesus' title as "The Word of God" refers to Him as the divine revelation of God Himself, God in human flesh.

John also used this phrase in John 1:1 when he said, "In the beginning was the Word, and the Word was with God, and the Word was God." Interestingly, John's record went back further than Genesis 1:1, for John talked about God's existence before creation.

Armies in Heaven

> **REVELATION 19:14**–"The armies in heaven, clothed in fine linen, white and clean, followed Him on white horses."

The "armies in heaven" wearing white will not be angels. They will be the same ones wearing white earlier in this chapter: the saints who have put on the righteousness of God.

> **REVELATION 19:8**–"To her it was granted to be arrayed in fine linen, clean and bright, for the fine linen is the righteous acts of the saints."

Armageddon

> **REVELATION 19:15a**–"Now out of His mouth goes a sharp sword, that with it He should strike the nations."

Jesus will judge the nations that have gathered for Armageddon against Him and His people Israel. Then He will establish His rule.

Rod of Iron

REVELATION 19:15b–"He Himself will rule them with a rod of iron."

Jesus references this rod of iron earlier in His letter to Thyatira and in a messianic psalm. This rod is a picture of the prophesied rule of our Lord.

> **Revelation 2:27**—"'He shall rule them with a rod of iron; they shall be dashed to pieces like the potter's vessels'—as I also have received from My Father."
>
> **Psalm 2:7-9**—"I will declare the decree: The LORD has said to Me, 'You are My Son, today I have begotten You. Ask of Me, and I will give You the nations for Your inheritance, and the ends of the earth for Your possession. You shall break them with a rod of iron; You shall dash them to pieces like a potter's vessel.'"

Winepress of Wrath

Before Jesus establishes His rule on Earth, He will crush His enemies like grapes in a winepress.

REVELATION 19:15c–"He Himself treads the winepress of the fierceness and wrath of Almighty God."

This is the reason Jesus wore a "robe dipped in blood," as verse 13 states. Isaiah prophesies about this day too.

> **Isaiah 63:1-2**—"Who is this who comes from Edom, with dyed garments from Bozrah, this One who is glorious in His apparel, traveling in the greatness of His strength? —'I who speak in righteousness, mighty to save.' Why is Your apparel red, and Your garments like one who treads in the winepress?"

See how God will wear red after treading in the winepress? The following verses explain this:

> **Isaiah 63:3-6**—"I have trodden the winepress alone, and from the peoples no one was with Me. For I have trodden them in My anger, and trampled them in My fury; their blood is sprinkled upon My garments, and I have stained all My robes. For the day of vengeance is in My heart, and the year of My redeemed has come. I looked, but there was no one to help, and I wondered that there was no one to uphold; therefore My own arm brought salvation for Me; and My own fury, it sustained Me. I have trodden down the peoples in My anger, made them drunk in My fury, and brought down their strength to the earth."

Conquering King

> **REVELATION 19:16**–"He has on His robe and on His thigh a name written: KING OF KINGS AND LORD OF LORDS."

Yes, Jesus will have a tattoo. His name will be written across His thigh. For people wondering if tattoos are okay, all I can say is Jesus will have one.

Supper of the Great God

> **REVELATION 19:17**–"I saw an angel standing in the sun; and he cried with a loud voice, saying to all the birds that fly in the midst of heaven, 'Come and gather together for the supper of the great God.'"

This angel is not Jesus, but a messenger angel told to summon vultures to come devour the flesh of those who fell in the battle.

And the angel called this "the supper of the great God." Note, the first supper of God will be one of joy (Revelation 19:9); the second supper, one of judgment.

Flesh of All

"Flesh" is mentioned five times in these last few verses, speaking not only of the literal flesh of people, but also the sinful nature that led them to their demise.

When God judges the world, no class will be spared. Among the fallen there will be kings, captains, mighty men, horses, all people free and slave, and all people small and great:

> **REVELATION 19:18**—"That you may eat the flesh of kings, the flesh of captains, the flesh of mighty men, the flesh of horses and of those who sit on them, and the flesh of all people, free and slave, both small and great."

The good news is that, just as God judges all sinners without discrimination, God shows mercy without discrimination to all sinners who repent.

Revelation 19 paints a gruesome scene, but those who will die did not need to! Anyone who repents will escape this judgment.

Summary of Jesus' Victory

> **REVELATION 19:19**—"I saw the beast, the kings of the earth, and their armies, gathered together to make war against Him who sat on the horse and against His army."

After describing the supper of the great God, John summarized what just happened: The beast and his armies made up of various nations will have gathered to fight against "Him who sat on the horse"—that is, God—"and against His army"—that is, the church.

REVELATION 19:20-21—"The beast was captured, and with him the false prophet who worked signs in his presence, by which he deceived those who received the mark of the beast and those who worshiped his image. These two were cast alive into the lake of fire burning with brimstone. And the rest were killed with the sword which proceeded from the mouth of Him who sat on the horse. And all the birds were filled with their flesh."

John repeated how the battle of Armageddon will end, with Jesus casting the Antichrist and the False Prophet into the lake of fire.

Some people think that the lake of fire will lead to annihilation, as if those who end up there burn up and are gone forever. But the Bible tells us that every soul lives forever, and the difference is where that soul ends up for all eternity.

> **Revelation 20:10**—"The devil, who deceived them, was cast into the lake of fire and brimstone where the beast and the false prophet are. And they will be tormented day and night forever and ever."

As the passage clarifies, neither hell nor the lake of fire are about annihilation, but perpetual suffering, and there, the Antichrist and all those who reject Christ will be punished.

Mount of Olives

The Bible not only tells us that Jesus will come down to battle against the armies of the Antichrist, but also that He will descend at the Mount of Olives.

> **Zechariah 14:4**—"In that day His feet will stand on the Mount of Olives, which faces Jerusalem on the east. And the Mount of Olives shall be split in two, from east to west, making a very large valley; half of the mountain shall move toward the north and half of it toward the south."

That Jesus will descend at the Mount of Olives is consistent with what the angels said at Jesus' ascension.

> **Acts 1:10-12**—"While they looked steadfastly toward heaven as He went up, behold, two men stood by them in white apparel, who also said, 'Men of Galilee, why do you stand gazing up into heaven? This same Jesus, who was taken up from you into heaven, will so come in like manner as you saw Him go into heaven.'
>
> "Then they returned to Jerusalem from the mount called Olivet, which is near Jerusalem, a Sabbath day's journey."

Thus, we know that when Jesus returns, He will touch down on the Mount of Olives in Jerusalem.

It Will Be Light

Zechariah said in that day, the evening will be light everywhere in the world.

> **Zechariah 14:6-7**—"It shall come to pass in that day that there will be no light; the lights will diminish. It shall be one day which is known to the LORD—neither day nor night. But at evening time it shall happen that it will be light."

Every Eye

Every eye will see Jesus in that day. We do not know if this will occur through technology or some divine miracle, but there will be no denying Him.

> **Zechariah 12:10**—"I will pour on the house of David and on the inhabitants of Jerusalem the Spirit of grace and supplication; then they will look on Me [Jesus] whom they pierced. Yes, they will mourn for Him as one mourns for his only son, and grieve for Him as one grieves for a firstborn."

Revelation says the same.

> **Revelation 1:7**—"Behold, He is coming with clouds, and every eye will see Him, even they who pierced Him. And all the tribes of the earth will mourn because of Him. Even so, Amen."

First and Second Coming

At His first coming, Jesus came gentle, riding on a donkey, and wept over the people's stubborn hearts. At His second coming, Jesus will come to judge, riding on a white horse.

At His first coming, Jesus wore a crown of thorns. At His second, Jesus will wear many royal crowns.

At His first coming, Jesus died on the cross to reconcile His enemies to Himself. At His second, Jesus will come as conqueror to judge those who have rejected His peace and chosen to be His enemies.

At His first coming, Jesus' blood was on His enemies. At His second, their blood will stain His robe. In that day, no one will be able to deny the deity of Christ any longer.

> **Philippians 2:8**—"Being found in appearance as a man, He humbled Himself and became obedient to the point of death, even the death of the cross."

Every knee will bow, so you can either bow now to your Savior, or then to your Judge. Everyone must choose.

Reflections on Revelation 19

Getting Started

In Revelation 19, after a hard seven years of tribulation, God will put an end to the corrupt and evil systems of the world (Revelation 19:19-21). How should the eventual coming of God's judgment influence our perspective (See Psalm 73:16-17; Revelation 19:2)?

Study Questions

1. What do the original Greek manuscripts emphasize in Revelation 19:1, and why?
2. God fulfills in Revelation 19 what He promised to the saints in Revelation 6:9-10. What attributes of God does this judgment reveal (see Deuteronomy 32:4; Proverbs 17:5; 22:22-23; Isaiah 25:1)? How can we respond to and rest in these attributes of God (see 2 Corinthians 7:1; Hebrews 6:10-12; 2 Peter 1:4; 1 John 1:9)?
3. How do Jewish betrothals in John's time parallel the relationship between Jesus and His church (see John 14:2; 1 Corinthians 6:20; Ephesians 1:7, 14)?
4. How does a Jewish groom's return illustrate Christ's second coming (see John 14:3)?
5. How does the Jewish banquet, concluding with the groom bringing his bride to his father's house and the consummation of their marriage, relate to how Jesus treats His bride, the church, in Revelation 19:7-9?
6. Why does the Bible portray the church as the bride of Christ, and why are we able to be dressed in white (see Romans 13:12; Revelation 3:4-5; 7:13-14; 19:7-9, 14)? What does the

believers' attire say about how Jesus views His people (see Ephesians 1:6)?

7. How does Jesus' second coming (Revelation 19:11) contrast with His first coming, and how does our response to His offer of salvation change which side of Him we will see (see Jonah 2:8; Luke 20:9-18; Romans 5:1; 1 Peter 2:4-9)?
8. Why is Jesus called the Word of God (see John 1:1; 14:9; Revelation 19:13)? How does this title harken back to the purpose of the book of Revelation (see Revelation 1:1)?
9. What do the winepress and the robe dipped in blood symbolize (Isaiah 63:1-6; Revelation 19:13, 15)? If Jesus will gain victory over the earth on His own (see Isaiah 63:3), why are the saints following behind Jesus in Revelation 19:14 (see 1 Thessalonians 4:17; 5:9-10)?
10. What is the "supper of the great God" described in Revelation 19:17, and how does it differ from the supper of verse 9?
11. How are men able to avoid the second supper of the great God if even the rich of the earth cannot escape this judgment (Revelation 19:18)? And what does this tell us about God's character (see Acts 10:34; Romans 2:11)?

Important Takeaways for Us Today

1. How has having a relationship with the Source of all virtue (see Acts 4:13; Romans 8:10-11; 2 Corinthians 3:18; Revelation 19:1) changed you?
2. How should we live, knowing that we are the bride of Christ (see Matthew 25:1-13; 2 Corinthians 11:2)?
3. When John worshipped the angel who showed him visions, the angel corrected him, saying they were both servants of God (Revelation 19:10). How do we avoid a mindset that elevates the messenger over God and His message (see 1 Corinthians 1:12-13; 3:1-7)?

20

The Prince of Peace

REVELATION 20

Can you imagine 1,000 years of peace here on Earth under our Lord's rule? Some people believe this number is figurative. Still others believe Jesus will not usher in the millennium, but rather, come at the end. But I hold to the premillennial view, in which Jesus binds up Satan and ushers in a reign of peace on Earth that lasts 1,000 years. Let's discuss why.

Three Views on the Millennium

Amillennial View

People who hold this view believe there will be no literal 1,000-year reign, but rather, that a figurative millennium began at the start of the church age. They also believe that Satan is currently bound, and that the tribulation is still to come along with the judgment that follows.

The problem with this view is the idea that Satan is already bound in spite of how crazy and sinful the world is. If he is already bound, we are in big trouble!

Proponents of this view include Augustine, the Roman Catholic Church, and some Baptists.

Postmillennial View

People who hold this view believe that Christ will return after the millennium, hence the *post* in postmillennial. To them, the 1,000 years is a literal time during which the greatest harvest for Christ occurs.

The problem with this theory is that the Bible does not teach that there will be a vast number of converts before Jesus' return, but rather, a great apostasy. While there will be a great advancement of the gospel—perhaps because of technology and transportation—the hearts of many will grow cold.

> Matthew 24:12-14—"Because lawlessness will abound, the love of many will grow cold. But he who endures to the end shall be saved. And this gospel of the kingdom will be preached in all the world as a witness to all the nations, and then the end will come."

Premillennial View

People who hold this view believe that Jesus will come to Earth at the end of the tribulation, conquer the Antichrist's armies in Armageddon, and then usher in the millennium, hence the *pre* in premillennial. This is the belief I hold.

Satan Bound

Bottomless Pit

> **REVELATION 20:1**–"Then I saw an angel coming down from heaven, having the key to the bottomless pit and a great chain in his hand."

"Then I saw" is a phrase John used five times in chapter 20. It is used to signify the beginning of a vision, and in this vision, John saw an angel who was given authority to hold the key to "the bottomless pit," or as the NIV translation says, "the abyss." Both words are translated from the same Greek word, *abyssos*, which is where we get our English word *abyss*.

The term "abyss" is only used nine times in the Bible: one time in Luke, and eight times in Revelation.

> **Luke 8:30-31**—"Jesus asked him, saying, 'What is your name?' And he said, 'Legion,' because many demons had entered him. And they begged Him that He would not command them to go out into the abyss."

The "abyss," or *abyssos*, is where the worst demons go, and this is such a frightening place that other demons are terrified to go there.

> **Jude 1:6**—"The angels who did not keep their proper domain, but left their own abode, He has reserved in everlasting chains under darkness for the judgment of the great day."

We know that there are demons in the world, but God, in His mercy, keeps the worst of the demons from us till the day of judgment.

Names of Satan

> **REVELATION 20:2**–"He laid hold of the dragon, that serpent of old, who is the Devil and Satan, and bound him for a thousand years."

John used various appellations for Satan, almost as if to make sure we understand who is being bound.

"The dragon" is the name used to describe him in Revelation. "That serpent of old" references back to Genesis 3, the first time Satan is mentioned in the Bible, when he tempted Eve in the Garden of Eden. "The Devil," or *diabolos* in the Greek text, means "accuser." "Satan," or *śāṭān*, is the Hebrew name for him, and it means "adversary" or "enemy."

Satan Sealed for a Time

> **REVELATION 20:3**–"He cast him into the bottomless pit, and shut him up, and set a seal on him, so that he should deceive the nations no more till the thousand years were finished. But after these things he must be released for a little while."

As verses 7-8 say, Satan will not be permanently bound at this time. He "must be released" after the 1,000-year reign of Christ.

Christ's Millennial Reign

Saints Reign with Christ

> **REVELATION 20:4**–"I saw thrones, and they sat on them, and judgment was committed to them. Then I saw the souls of those who had been beheaded for their witness to Jesus and for the word of God, who had not worshiped the beast or his image, and had not received his mark on their foreheads or on their hands. And they lived and reigned with Christ for a thousand years."

The people who will sit on the thrones are the saints.

> **1 Corinthians 6:2a**—"Do you not know that the saints will judge the world?"

Jesus will give authority to believers who are resurrected at the rapture so that they may judge the world during the millennium.

Tribulation Saints

In the middle of verse 4, the Bible distinguishes between pre-tribulation believers and those who became believers during the tribulation with the phrase "then I saw."

John saw this group of tribulation martyrs earlier in Revelation.

> **Revelation 15:2-3a**—"I saw something like a sea of glass"—the "sea" being a crowd of people—"mingled with fire, and those who have the victory over the beast, over his image and over his mark and over the number of his name, standing on the sea of glass, having harps of God. They sing the song of Moses, the servant of God, and the song of the Lamb."

Remember, despite how miserable the earth can get, those who call on the name of the Lord will be saved and their reward in heaven will be great.

> **Romans 8:18**—"I consider that the sufferings of this present time are not worthy to be compared with the glory which shall be revealed in us."

Hold on to this truth, for this is the hope of the church.

First Resurrection

> **REVELATION 20:5**–"The rest of the dead did not live again until the thousand years were finished. This is the first resurrection."

The "rest of the dead" are the ones who died in their unbelief.

This is why, in verse 6, those who rise in "the first resurrection" are blessed: The dead in Christ will live to reign with Him, and the rest of the dead, who will not rise until the second resurrection, are those who will have rejected the Savior.

> **REVELATION 20:6a**–"Blessed and holy is he who has part in the first resurrection."

Second Death

> **REVELATION 20:6b**–"Over such the second death has no power."

The "second death" is when God will judge unbelievers.

Priests of God

> **REVELATION 20:6c**–"They shall be priests of God and of Christ, and shall reign with Him a thousand years."

Christ will reign in Jerusalem, and the saints will reign with Him and be His priests during the millennium. This concept is reiterated throughout Revelation:

> **Revelation 1:5b-6**—"To Him who loved us and washed us from our sins in His own blood, and has made us kings and priests to His God and Father, to Him be glory and dominion forever and ever. Amen."
>
> **Revelation 5:9-10**—"They sang a new song, saying:
>
> "You are worthy to take the scroll, and to open its seals; for You were slain, and have redeemed us to God by Your blood out of every tribe and tongue and people and nation, and have made us kings and priests to our God; and we shall reign on the earth."

As priests, we will serve Jesus and represent Him to the people on Earth during the millennium.

In the Old Testament, priests represented man to God and God to man. But the New Testament gave us Christ, our Great High Priest, so we no longer need intermediaries between God and man, for that role is fulfilled in Christ. However, while we are not priests in the Old Testament sense of representing man to God, we are still priests of God in the sense that we will represent who God is to those around us.

This priesthood role will be given to both glorified and unglorified believers during the millennium because there will be those who will be saved during the tribulation, survive, and go into the millennium. Not yet in their glorified bodies, they will have children and grandchildren, and all of those new generations will need to know Christ. Remember that even though Jesus will be on the throne, the living will still be tempted by their own flesh. Although Satan's imprisonment will make godliness easier, the living will still have a sin nature. There will still be people who need to hear about Jesus during the millennium and to trust Him as Lord and Savior.

Wicked Judged

Not everybody who will survive the tribulation will be right with God. First, Jesus will separate *to* Him the sheep—that is, the believers.

> **Matthew 25:32-34**—"All the nations will be gathered before Him, and He will separate them one from another, as a shepherd divides his sheep from the goats. And He will set the sheep on His right hand, but the goats on the left. Then the King will say to those on His right hand, 'Come, you blessed of My Father, inherit the kingdom prepared for you from the foundation of the world.'"

Then, Jesus will separate *from* Him the goats—the unbelievers.

> **Matthew 25:41**—"He will also say to those on the left hand, 'Depart from Me, you cursed, into the everlasting fire prepared for the devil and his angels.'"

Millennium Characteristics

1. With Christ on the throne, there will be no more war.

> **Isaiah 2:2-5**—"Now it shall come to pass in the latter days that the mountain of the LORD's house shall be established on the top of the mountains, and shall be exalted above the hills; and all nations shall flow to it. Many people shall come

and say, 'Come, and let us go up to the mountain of the Lord, to the house of the God of Jacob; He will teach us His ways, and we shall walk in His paths.' For out of Zion shall go forth the law, and the word of the Lord from Jerusalem. He shall judge between the nations, and rebuke many people; they shall beat their swords into plowshares, and their spears into pruning hooks; nation shall not lift up sword against nation, neither shall they learn war anymore.

"O house of Jacob, come and let us walk in the light of the Lord."

2. Animals will also live at peace, with each other and with man—just as in preflood days.

Isaiah 11:1-10—"There shall come forth a Rod from the stem of Jesse, and a Branch shall grow out of his roots. The Spirit of the Lord shall rest upon Him, the Spirit of wisdom and understanding, the Spirit of counsel and might, the Spirit of knowledge and of the fear of the Lord.

"His delight is in the fear of the Lord, and He shall not judge by the sight of His eyes, nor decide by the hearing of His ears; but with righteousness He shall judge the poor, and decide with equity for the meek of the earth; He shall strike the earth with the rod of His mouth, and with the breath of His lips He shall slay the wicked. Righteousness shall be the belt of His loins, and faithfulness the belt of His waist.

"The wolf also shall dwell with the lamb, the leopard shall lie down with the young goat, the calf and the young lion and the fatling together; and a little child shall lead them. The cow and the bear shall graze; their young ones shall lie down together; and the lion shall eat straw like the ox. The nursing child shall play by the cobra's hole, and the weaned child shall put his hand in the viper's den. They shall not hurt nor destroy in all My holy mountain, for the earth shall be full of the knowledge of the Lord as the waters cover the sea.

"'And in that day there shall be a Root of Jesse, who shall stand as a banner to the people; for the Gentiles shall seek Him, and His resting place shall be glorious.'"

3. People will enjoy long lives.

Isaiah 65:19-25—"'I will rejoice in Jerusalem, and joy in My people; the voice of weeping shall no longer be heard in her, nor the voice of crying.

"'No more shall an infant from there live but a few days, nor an old man who has not fulfilled his days; for the child shall die one hundred years old, but the sinner being one hundred years old shall be accursed. They shall build houses and inhabit them; they shall plant vineyards and eat their fruit. They shall not build and another inhabit; they shall not plant and another eat; for as the days of a tree, so shall be the days of My people, and My elect shall long enjoy the work of their hands. They shall not labor in vain, nor bring forth children for trouble; for they shall be the descendants of the blessed of the Lord, and their offspring with them.

"'It shall come to pass that before they call, I will answer; and while they are still speaking, I will hear. The wolf and the lamb shall feed together, the lion shall eat straw like the ox, and dust shall be the serpent's food. They shall not hurt nor destroy in all My holy mountain,' says the Lord."

Many factors that may decrease a person's lifespan will be removed, and with Jesus as King, much will change and improve in our world to the point that people will consider dying at 100 years to be dying young.

4. People will worship Jesus in Jerusalem.

> **Zechariah 14:16-21**—"It shall come to pass that everyone who is left of all the nations which came against Jerusalem shall go up from year to year to worship the King, the Lord of hosts, and to keep the Feast of Tabernacles. And it shall be that whichever of the families of the earth do not come up to Jerusalem to worship the King, the Lord of hosts, on them there will be no rain. If the family of Egypt will not come up and enter in, they shall have no rain; they shall receive the plague with which the Lord strikes the nations who do not come up to keep the Feast of Tabernacles. This shall be the punishment of Egypt and the punishment of all the nations that do not come up to keep the Feast of Tabernacles.
>
> "In that day 'HOLINESS TO THE LORD' shall be engraved on the bells of the horses. The pots in the Lord's house shall be like the bowls before the altar. Yes, every pot in Jerusalem and Judah shall be holiness to the Lord of hosts. Everyone who sacrifices shall come and take them and cook in them. In that day there shall no longer be a Canaanite in the house of the Lord of hosts."

Interestingly, we will again celebrate Jewish feasts. But this time, the feasts will not be looking forward to the coming of Messiah, but rather, looking back to the salvation Jesus provided. This echoes what we do for communion today: We look back at the sacrifice of Christ.

Satanic Rebellion

Satan Released

> **REVELATION 20:7**–"Now when the thousand years have expired, Satan will be released from his prison."

When Satan is bound, those on Earth will live in a utopian society, with the only imperfection being man's own fleshly bent toward sin.

Therefore, at the end of the millennium, Satan will be released to give people a choice as to whom they will serve. What is so unfortunate is that many will choose to gather against the Lord, freely turning their backs on the One who showed them mercy and grace.

Nations Deceived

> **REVELATION 20:8**–"[Satan] will go out to deceive the nations which are in the four corners of the earth, Gog and Magog, to gather them together to battle, whose number is as the sand of the sea."

This army's rise reveals the wickedness of the human heart and the powerful delusion of Satan. The Bible records the two factors that will come together to create a large-scale rebellion made up of people whose number will be "as the sand of the sea."

And again, we see the mention of "Gog and Magog." Some believe this refers to the advancement of Russia prophesied in Ezekiel 38–39, but they are not the same event. The Ezekiel 38–39 prophecy describes wars leading up to and culminating with Armageddon, while the Revelation 20 prophecy describes a conflict happening after the millennium. Although the Gog and Magog in Revelation 20 may refer to Russia as well, it is not referencing Ezekiel's prophecy.

Fire from God

> **REVELATION 20:9**–"They went up on the breadth of the earth and surrounded the camp of the saints and the beloved city. And fire came down from God out of heaven and devoured them."

Satan and his rebellion will try to advance against God, but despite their numbers, God will quickly quench their attempted coup with fire.

Here are some lessons from Satan's failed rebellion:

1. The heart of man is depraved. Even when living under King Jesus and enjoying the peace He brings, men still would rather fight against God alongside Satan than submit to God.

   Jeremiah 17:9—"The heart is deceitful above all things, and desperately wicked; who can know it?"

2. Satan is powerfully deceptive. He will lure many away even in a near-perfect world.
3. God is just in His judgments. When Jesus reigns on Earth, He will bring peace and prosperity with Him, but even then, people will still rebel. This proves God is just in His judgments.

Lake of Fire

> **REVELATION 20:10**—"The devil, who deceived them, was cast into the lake of fire and brimstone where the beast and the false prophet are. And they will be tormented day and night forever and ever."

Initially, Satan was put into the abyss, while the Antichrist and False Prophet were cast into the lake of fire.

> **Revelation 19:20**—"Then the beast was captured, and with him the false prophet who worked signs in his presence, by which he deceived those who received the mark of the beast and those who worshiped his image. These two were cast alive into the lake of fire burning with brimstone."

But after Satan's last attempt at a coup against God, he, too, will be cast into the lake of fire, the final place of judgment and perpetual torment.

Eternal Judgment

Jesus referred to this lake of fire 11 times in the Gospels using the Aramaic word *Gehinnom* (or *Gehenna* in the Greek), and then described the place with the phrase "forever and ever" in Revelation 20:10. This phrase debunks the unbiblical doctrine of annihilation.

The Bible says the soul is eternal, but whether a soul spends eternity with or without God depends on each man's response to Jesus—not a predestined call to heaven or hell.

> **John 3:16**—"God so loved the world that He gave His only begotten Son, that whoever believes in Him should not perish but have everlasting life."

God's invitation is to "whoever." You will end up in heaven or hell based on your choice.

Despite the Bible's clear stance, in 2018, Pope Francis gave an interview to editor Eugenio Scalfari, saying that bad souls "are not punished…Those who do not repent and cannot be forgiven disappear. A hell doesn't exist, the disappearance of sinning souls exists."[1]

Conservative Irish Catholic Patrick Buchanan wrote an opinion piece for *Newsmax* wherein he disagreed with Francis, calling his stance an unbiblical view.[2] And we can rightly discern between these beliefs because we know the Bible to be true, inerrant, and more authoritative than any man's opinion.

Great White Throne

Have you heard someone say, "Only God can judge me"? Well, here is the part where He does just that. And let me tell you, this is not a judgment you want to be part of. No one there will be found guiltless, hence Jesus says, "Blessed and holy is he who has part in the first resurrection. Over such the second death has no power, but they shall be priests of God and of Christ, and shall reign with Him a thousand years" (Revelation 20:6). And at this fierce judgment, heaven and Earth will flee away—how amazing is our God!

Unbelievers Judged

The great white throne judgment is for unbelievers—not believers. The saints will not be a part of this judgment, for either they will have died and joined Jesus, ruling and reigning with Him, or they will have been spared, according to Matthew 25:33-40, for being sheep rather than goats.

When we put Matthew 25 together with Revelation 20, we can conclude that Jesus will judge the unrighteous and allow the righteous to enter the millennium. The first generation of those in Christ's kingdom will all be Christians.

Believers will already be judged righteous through Christ's blood. All that will be left will be for Jesus to judge unbelievers.

But the great white throne judgment is not to determine unbelievers' guilt, but rather, to review their works with them and show them why they will be condemned.

Heavens Fled Away

Heaven and earth will flee from God's presence, making way for a new heaven and earth.

> **REVELATION 20:11**–"I saw a great white throne and Him who sat on it, from whose face the earth and the heaven fled away. And there was found no place for them."

This unmaking and remaking is predicted throughout Scripture.

> **Matthew 24:35**—"Heaven and earth will pass away, but My words will by no means pass away."
>
> **2 Peter 3:7**—"The heavens and the earth which are now preserved by the same word, are reserved for fire until the day of judgment and perdition of ungodly men."
>
> **2 Peter 3:10-13**—"The day of the Lord will come as a thief in the night, in which the heavens will pass away with a great noise, and the elements will melt with fervent heat; both the earth and the works that are in it will be burned up.

> Therefore, since all these things will be dissolved, what manner of persons ought you to be in holy conduct and godliness, looking for and hastening the coming of the day of God, because of which the heavens will be dissolved, being on fire, and the elements will melt with fervent heat? Nevertheless we, according to His promise, look for new heavens and a new earth in which righteousness dwells."

Standing Before God

> **REVELATION 20:12**–"I saw the dead, small and great, standing before God, and books were opened. And another book was opened, which is the Book of Life. And the dead were judged according to their works, by the things which were written in the books."

The dead will stand before God when there will be no Earth or heaven, suspended in the air as they await judgment.

God has books, and He will open them at the great white throne judgment. These books will include the following:

1. Bible

> **John 12:48**—"He who rejects Me, and does not receive My words, has that which judges him—the word that I have spoken will judge him in the last day."

2. Book of records

> **Psalm 139:16**—"Your eyes saw my substance, being yet unformed. And in Your book they all were written, the days fashioned for me, when as yet there were none of them."

3. Book of remembrance

> **Psalm 56:8**—"You number my wanderings; put my tears into Your bottle; are they not in Your book?"

God is not indifferent, but rather, records our sorrows with care. He is the God who sees.

> **Malachi 3:16**—"Then those who feared the LORD spoke to one another, and the LORD listened and heard them; so a book of remembrance was written before Him for those who fear the LORD and who meditate on His name."

4. Book of works

> **REVELATION 20:12c**–"The dead were judged according to their works, by the things which were written in the books."

This book will stand as a testimony against unbelievers.

5. Book of Life

> **REVELATION 20:12b**–"Another book was opened, which is the Book of Life."

The Book of Life is mentioned nine times in the Bible, and seven of these mentions are found in Revelation.

> **Philippians 4:3**—"I urge you also, true companion, help these women who labored with me in the gospel, with Clement also, and the rest of my fellow workers, whose names are in the Book of Life."

> **Psalm 69:28**—"Let them be blotted out of the book of the living, and not be written with the righteous."
>
> **Revelation 3:5**—"He who overcomes shall be clothed in white garments, and I will not blot out his name from the Book of Life; but I will confess his name before My Father and before His angels."

God's Provision for Children

Some wonder what happens to children who die too young to know right from wrong, and I believe that God has made gracious provision for them.

Exodus

The picture of salvation presented in Exodus seems to imply God will have mercy for those under the age of accountability. Looking at the account of the exodus through this lens, we can see that just as the Israelites left the slavery of Egypt for freedom in the Promised Land, Christians leave the slavery of sin for freedom in Christ. Also, as Israel did not enter the Promised Land with Moses, the representative of the law, we cannot enter heaven by keeping the law. Rather, we enter by faith in Jesus just as Israel entered the Promised Land under Joshua, who, like Jesus, has a name that means "Yahweh is salvation."

And just as disobedience was the only thing that kept Israel out of the Promised Land then, the disobedient rejection of Jesus keeps people from heaven now.

But God made gracious provision for the young generation of Israel who had not known better at the time their parents rebelled. He allowed the new generation to enter the Promised Land, though the disbelieving previous generation died in the wilderness (except for Joshua and Caleb):

> **Deuteronomy 1:39**—"Moreover your little ones and your children, who you say will be victims, who today have no

> knowledge of good and evil, they shall go in there; to them I will give it, and they shall possess it."

So perhaps God also makes gracious provision for children when they die before reaching the age of accountability.

David

David also suggests that children who are too young to understand good from evil may go to heaven, because when his infant son died, he prophesied that he would see him again.

> **2 Samuel 12:23**—"Now he is dead; why should I fast? Can I bring him back again? I shall go to him, but he shall not return to me."

The question becomes, When is a person's name written? I believe all our names are written at the beginning of our lives and blotted out only if we reject Jesus, hence why in Revelation 3:5 and Psalm 69:28, the Bible describes the evil getting "blotted out" of the Book of Life rather than the evil not being written into the Book of Life.

Dead at Sea

> **REVELATION 20:13**–"The sea gave up the dead who were in it, and Death and Hades delivered up the dead who were in them. And they were judged, each one according to his works."

For those who ask whether your relative's ashes that have been scattered at sea will be gathered up, here is your answer: "The sea gave up the dead who were in it."

Second Death

> **REVELATION 20:14-15**—"Then Death and Hades were cast into the lake of fire. This is the second death. And anyone not found written in the Book of Life was cast into the lake of fire."

In the second resurrection, "Death and Hades" will die, and their inhabitants will die a second death. This is what unbelievers will have chosen. God made provision for us, leaving us with the choice to accept or reject Jesus.

Reflections on Revelation 20

Getting Started

Of the three views on the millennium, which makes the most sense in the context of Matthew 24:12-14 and the continuing evil in the world? How does this view impact how you read Revelation and understand your place in the timeline of end-times events?

Study Questions

1. How is the abyss an example of God's mercy to those on Earth (see Luke 8:30-31; Jude 1:6)? How does this show of mercy inform your understanding of the dual roles of justice (see Deuteronomy 24:14-15; Romans 13:3-4)?
2. What kind of picture did John paint by using four names for Satan in Revelation 20:2? And why is Satan only bound "for a little while" (see Revelation 20:3, 7)?
3. Who are the "rest of the dead" (Revelation 20:5), and how do they contrast those who will be raised in the first resurrection (see Revelation 20:4)? How can we take hope from the future promised to those who die in Christ Jesus (see Romans 8:18)?
4. What is the second death, and how can that death be avoided (see John 5:24; Hebrews 9:27-28; Revelation 2:11; 20:6)?
5. Why will the saints take on a priestly role (see Revelation 1:5-6; 5:9-10) when Jesus will rule on Earth during the millennium (Revelation 20:6) and Satan will be bound? What does the need for priests during this time tell us about human nature? How should this affect our response to sin in our own lives (Jeremiah 17:9; Romans 7:18, 22-25; Galatians 5:16)?
6. What are the characteristics of the millennium (see Isaiah 2:2-5; 11:1-10; 65:19-25; Zechariah 14:16-21)? What are these

millennium characteristics directly opposite to (see Genesis 3:17-19; 6:3; 9:1-2; Romans 5:12-21)?

7. The millennium ends with Satan's release and the people of many nations joining him, deceived (Revelation 20:7-8). How is it that Satan will be able to fool men so easily when the same people will have experienced Jesus' perfect rule (see Proverbs 28:5; Jeremiah 17:9; 2 Timothy 4:3-4)?
8. Despite what the unbiblical doctrine of annihilation claims, what do Revelation 20:10 and John 3:16 say about the existence of the soul? How should the eternal nature of our souls affect how we view ourselves and others (see Matthew 10:28; Romans 10:14-15; 1 Corinthians 15:53-58; 1 Timothy 4:8)?
9. Why will unbelievers face the great white throne judgment if salvation comes by faith alone, and what will they be judged by (see Psalms 69:28; 139:16; Malachi 3:16; John 12:48; Philippians 4:3; Revelation 3:5; 20:12)?
10. How do the exodus story and the way David reacted to his child's death provide comfort to parents who have lost young children (see 2 Samuel 12:23)? What does this tell us about God's view of children too young to understand spiritual matters?

Important Takeaways for Us Today

1. Revelation 20:4 describes pre-tribulation believers sitting as judges under Christ. How does knowing your future role affect how you deal with conflicts (see 2 Corinthians 4:17-18)?
2. How is the rolling away of the heavens in Revelation 20:11 a reminder that God's Word is our sure foundation (see Matthew 24:35; 2 Peter 3:7, 10-13)? What foundation are we to build on, and what will endure (see Matthew 7:24-27; 1 Corinthians 3:11-15)?

21

A New Beginning

REVELATION 21

Remember how heaven and earth fled before God's white throne judgment in the previous chapter? Well, those who choose to believe in Jesus will not have to face God's wrath. Instead, they will get to enjoy the new heaven and earth that God creates. And unlike the millennium, this period will last for eternity future, and we will be with Christ forevermore.

A World Made New

New Heaven and Earth

> **REVELATION 21:1**—"Now I saw a new heaven and a new earth, for the first heaven and the first earth had passed away. Also there was no more sea."

John referenced the passing away of the old heaven and earth, which is mentioned in the previous chapter.

> **Revelation 20:11a**—"Then I saw a great white throne and Him who sat on it, from whose face the earth and the heaven fled away."

This means that the old will leave before the new can be established. Bible scholars believe that between one world's unmaking and the formation of the next, we will be held up in space as God creates all things new.

This is not too difficult for God.

> **Colossians 1:16-17**—"By Him all things were created that are in heaven and that are on earth, visible and invisible, whether thrones or dominions or principalities or powers. All things were created through Him and for Him. And He is before all things, and in Him all things consist."

Even now, if at any point Jesus releases His hold on Earth, everything would unwind. He holds it all together!

New Jerusalem Descends

> **REVELATION 21:2**–"I, John, saw the holy city, New Jerusalem, coming down out of heaven from God, prepared as a bride adorned for her husband."

The building of New Jerusalem was predicted.

> **Isaiah 65:17-19**—"Behold, I create new heavens and a new earth; and the former shall not be remembered or come to mind. But be glad and rejoice forever in what I create; for behold, I create Jerusalem as a rejoicing, and her people a joy. I will rejoice in Jerusalem, and joy in My people; the voice of weeping shall no longer be heard in her, nor the voice of crying."

> **2 Peter 3:10-13**—"The day of the Lord will come as a thief in the night, in which the heavens will pass away with a great noise, and the elements will melt with fervent heat; both the earth and the works that are in it will be burned up. Therefore, since all these things will be dissolved, what manner of persons ought you to be in holy conduct and godliness, looking for and hastening the coming of the day of God, because of which the heavens will be dissolved, being on fire, and the elements will melt with fervent heat? Nevertheless we, according to His promise, look for new heavens and a new earth in which righteousness dwells."

And New Jerusalem is beyond imagining. Picture a day with nothing to worry about, nothing decaying or dying, and everything joyous and good—even you! Not only that, but it will be beautiful like "a bride adorned for her husband"!

God with Man

Just as God used to walk with man in the Garden of Eden, He will do so again in the New Jerusalem.

> **REVELATION 21:3**–"I heard a loud voice from heaven saying, 'Behold, the tabernacle of God is with men, and He will dwell with them, and they shall be His people. God Himself will be with them and be their God.'"

The word "tabernacle" in Revelation is the same word for "dwelt" in John.

> **John 1:14**—"The Word became flesh and dwelt among us, and we beheld His glory, the glory as of the only begotten of the Father, full of grace and truth."

This is God dwelling with us, tabernacling with us.

Wipe Away Every Tear

> **REVELATION 21:4**–"God will wipe away every tear from their eyes; there shall be no more death, nor sorrow, nor crying. There shall be no more pain, for the former things have passed away."

Some ask whether we will remember our family members who did not accept Jesus. Sometimes memory is a great thing, and sometimes it is a terrible thing. Perhaps God, in His mercy, will take away the painful memories to spare us the hurt.

He will also take away the sinful memories, and in heaven, no one will be dwelling on their past mistakes. Rather, we will be fixated on God's presence, and He will make all things new.

But then why is Jesus wiping away tears? Perhaps we will be crying in relief, glad that every burden we carried in life is finally done away with!

All Things New

> **REVELATION 21:5**–"He who sat on the throne said, 'Behold, I make all things new.' And He said to me, 'Write, for these words are true and faithful.'"

This is not a redesign of Earth. No, all will be made new.

Ages in Heaven

In heaven, there will not be feeble people shuffling around in walkers. While the Bible is silent on the specifics, some speculate that heaven will have a universal age of 30. This thought comes from Numbers 4:3, which states that the minimum age for priests was age 30.

Besides this, Saul and David became kings at 30, Jesus' public ministry began at age 30, and even Adam is speculated by rabbis to have been created with the physical age of 30.

Some wonder whether children who die young will likely be part of this "universal age." Regardless, we will know and recognize our loved ones because "now [we] know in part; then [we] shall know fully, even as [we] have been fully known" (1 Corinthians 13:12 ESV).

The truth is, we do not really know what to expect. But one thing is certain—the new world will be far better than, and not worth comparing to, life on Earth!

My Son

> **REVELATION 21:6-7**—"He said to me, 'It is done! I am the Alpha and the Omega, the Beginning and the End. I will give of the fountain of the water of life freely to him who thirsts. He who overcomes shall inherit all things, and I will be his God and he shall be My son.'"

"Son" in this passage is a generic term, including both sons and daughters of God.

Unbelievers Absent

> **REVELATION 21:8**—"The cowardly, unbelieving, abominable, murderers, sexually immoral, sorcerers, idolaters, and all liars shall have their part in the lake which burns with fire and brimstone, which is the second death."
>
> **REVELATION 21:27**—"There shall by no means enter it anything that defiles, or causes an abomination or a lie, but only those who are written in the Lamb's Book of Life."

Unbelievers will be absent from the kingdom by their own choices. Only believers may enjoy New Jerusalem.

New Jerusalem

Light of God

> **REVELATION 21:10-11**–"He carried me away in the Spirit to a great and high mountain, and showed me the great city, the holy Jerusalem, descending out of heaven from God, having the glory of God. Her light was like a most precious stone, like a jasper stone, clear as crystal."

New Jerusalem will have no sun or moon. Light will come directly from God, a truth that is repeated at the end of the chapter.

> **REVELATION 21:23**–"The city had no need of the sun or of the moon to shine in it, for the glory of God illuminated it. The Lamb is its light."

Effects of a Sunless Sky

Some scholars believe the word "need" signifies New Jerusalem will be bright enough that it will not require a sun or moon, but not that these celestial bodies will not be there. But if they are not needed, there is no reason for God to put them in the sky.

Assuming the Lord will be the only light of the world, we can speculate on some of the new Earth's atmospheric conditions. Constant light means there will be no night. God's glory will continually shine on us.

And we will have no need for rest like we do now. Our current bodies need to regenerate during the night, but our glorified bodies will not be subject to decay. Sleep cycles will become unnecessary. New Jerusalem will be the real city that never sleeps.

The temperature will also be perfectly regulated by Jesus.

For our current Earth, the moon regulates the ocean tides. The moon's presence makes sense now as 70 percent of Earth is covered with water, but on the new Earth, there will be "no more sea" (Revelation

21:1). There will only be a freshwater river that I will mention when we look at Revelation 22.

Of course, no sea means no beach, but we will not care on that day. We will not need anything of the old Earth, for God will make everything better, and all our desire will be fixed on Him.

Twelve Gates

> **REVELATION 21:12-13**–"Also she had a great and high wall with twelve gates, and twelve angels at the gates, and names written on them, which are the names of the twelve tribes of the children of Israel: three gates on the east, three gates on the north, three gates on the south, and three gates on the west."

In the Old Testament, the encampment of Israel was configured according to tribe. Perhaps the gates of New Jerusalem will be laid out according to this configuration. If that is the case, then Judah, Issachar, and Zebulun will be at the east side of the city; Gad, Simeon, and Reuben at the south; Ephraim, Manasseh, and Benjamin at the west; and Naphtali, Asher, and Dan at the north.

Twelve Foundations

> **REVELATION 21:14**–"Now the wall of the city had twelve foundations, and on them were the names of the twelve apostles of the Lamb."

"The Lamb" is the title Jesus uses most throughout Revelation, and this is the title John chose to describe the God-Man Christ Jesus, whom the apostles belonged to. These 12 apostles' names will be written on the 12 foundations, or layers, of the city walls. Judas of course will be omitted, so I speculate that Paul will be the twelfth apostle listed.

The foundations and gates are named to honor history, and they prove that God is not done with Israel.

Tour of Jerusalem

> **REVELATION 21:15**–"He who talked with me had a gold reed to measure the city, its gates, and its wall."

The "he" who spoke with John was one of the seven angels who had one of the seven bowls of judgment.

> **REVELATION 21:9**–"One of the seven angels who had the seven bowls filled with the seven last plagues came to me and talked with me, saying, 'Come, I will show you the bride, the Lamb's wife.'"

This same angel took John on a tour of the heavenly city:

> **REVELATION 21:16**–"The city is laid out as a square; its length is as great as its breadth. And he measured the city with the reed: twelve thousand furlongs. Its length, breadth, and height are equal."

Measurements

New Jerusalem is described as a cube: The city's length, breadth, and height are equal. And the place will be large because it measures 12,000 furlongs—or 12,000 stadia in the NIV and ESV—which is roughly 1,500 miles in every direction. That is the distance between Virginia and Colorado.

To give you some perspective, the old city of Jerusalem is currently only one mile in every direction, but New Jerusalem will be roughly the size of the moon.

Population

Dr. Henry Morris, the founder of The Institute for Creation Research and former department chair of civil engineering at Virginia Tech, made some calculations and determined that the past, present, and future people on Earth add up to about 100 billion. He estimated that if 20 percent of that 100 billion accepted Jesus as their Savior, 20 billion people will be in the New Jerusalem.[1]

That sounds crowded, but because the city is described as a cube, the city block will likely not be a square block, but a cube block. This means there will probably be vertical as well as horizontal structures. That is more than enough space to accommodate 20 billion people.

Walls

The New Jerusalem wall will be approximately 200 feet thick!

REVELATION 21:17–"Then he measured its wall: one hundred and forty-four cubits, according to the measure of a man, that is, of an angel."

Though there will be no need for walls because God has already dealt with His enemies, the purpose of these walls will likely be to define the boundaries of New Jerusalem.

Every Precious Stone

New Jerusalem will be made with every precious stone.

REVELATION 21:18–"The construction of its wall was of jasper; and the city was pure gold, like clear glass."

REVELATION 21:21b–"The street of the city was pure gold, like transparent glass."

Gold will be transparent rather than opaque, for the glory of God will shine through every part of this city.

Twelve Gemstones

> **REVELATION 21:19-20**—"The foundations of the wall of the city were adorned with all kinds of precious stones: the first foundation was jasper, the second sapphire, the third chalcedony, the fourth emerald, the fifth sardonyx, the sixth sardius, the seventh chrysolite, the eighth beryl, the ninth topaz, the tenth chrysoprase, the eleventh jacinth, and the twelfth amethyst."

Some try to make a correlation between these precious stones and the high priest's ephod vestment, but only eight of the 12 gemstones mentioned are identical to the gems that adorned the priest's vestment, so this is a hard correlation to make.

Here are the colors of the 12 foundation stones that Revelation describes:

1. The first foundation is jasper. Gemologists differ in how they define various gemstones, and jasper is one of them, for while jasper is a multicolored gem in the class of quartz and is usually reddish from iron oxide, others argue that jasper can also be white, yellow, green, or orange.
2. The second foundation layer is sapphire, which is a clear, deep blue.
3. The third is chalcedony, a greenish stone with stripes of other colors mixed in.
4. The fourth is emerald, a dark, rich green.
5. The fifth is sardonyx, a reddish-white onyx like the color of healthy fingernails.

6. The sixth is sardius, a fiery red stone. Sardius was the first stone on the priest's ephod; it represented the tribe of Reuben.
7. The seventh is chrysolite, a bright, light green.
8. The eighth is beryl, a sea-green emerald that is lighter than chalcedony.
9. The ninth is topaz, a transparent, greenish-yellow stone.
10. The tenth is chrysoprase, a yellowish, pale-green color that is like aquamarine.
11. The eleventh is jacinth, a violet, hyacinth gem.
12. And the twelfth is amethyst, a purple stone.

New Colors

Here is where things get interesting: We have three primary colors from which all other colors are derived. Imagine if there was just one more primary color—it would make possible another host of colors that we cannot even imagine!

There are 1,000 shades of visible light, and within those, we can detect 100 different levels of red-green shades and 100 levels of yellow-blue shades. And when you take 1,000 times 100 times 100, the human eye can see 10 million different shades of color. So, if there were just one more primary color, think of the millions of new colors that would exist. We would be putting on colorblind glasses as we step into New Jerusalem.

Pearly Gates

> **REVELATION 21:21a**—"The twelve gates were twelve pearls: each individual gate was of one pearl."

That is a big pearl!

No Temple

> **REVELATION 21:22**—"I saw no temple in it, for the Lord God Almighty and the Lamb are its temple."

No temple will be necessary because God will dwell among us. He will be the temple.

> **Revelation 22:4a**—"They shall see His face."
>
> **1 Corinthians 13:12**—"Now we see in a mirror, dimly, but then face to face. Now I know in part, but then I shall know just as I also am known."

God is not a recluse, but rather, will reveal Himself to us.

There will also be no temple because there will be no need for sacrifices: All the inhabitants are redeemed. There will be no rebellion—at least among us (some believe the angels will still be able to rebel). And we will not need a central place of worship, for we will worship God everywhere and always.

The Nations

> **REVELATION 21:24**—"The nations of those who are saved shall walk in its light, and the kings of the earth bring their glory and honor into it."
>
> **REVELATION 21:26**—"They shall bring the glory and the honor of the nations into it."

"Nations" can be translated as "Gentiles." This signifies that New Jerusalem is a place made not just for the Jews, but also the Gentiles.

Now, we do not know why kings and nations are delineated here. The meaning is not clear, but we will find out when we get there.

No Night

> **REVELATION 21:25**—"Its gates shall not be shut at all by day (there shall be no night there)."

Again, God is constantly illuminating the city.

Reflections on Revelation 21

Getting Started

When touring New Jerusalem, John gave a detailed account of God's beautiful city (Revelation 21:2, 9-26). How does this description correspond with the nature of our God (see Psalm 27:4; Isaiah 33:17; Matthew 10:29; 1 Corinthians 14:33)?

Study Questions

1. Why will heaven and earth flee before God's presence (see Revelation 20:11; 21:1)? How does God do a similar miracle in believers' lives (see 1 Corinthians 6:9-11; 2 Corinthians 5:17-18; Ephesians 4:17-24)?
2. What is the significance of the word "tabernacle" in Revelation 21:3 (see John 1:14)? In what ways can this truth influence us (see Psalm 118:6; Isaiah 41:10; John 14:15-21; Philippians 4:6-7; Hebrews 13:5)?
3. There is speculation about whether we will remember the sorrows of our pasts; how does Revelation 21:4 contribute to this conversation?
4. Who will be absent from New Jerusalem (Revelation 21:8, 27) and why (see John 3:16-18; Hebrews 3:15-19; 4:1-3)?
5. Why will there be no sun and moon in the new world (Revelation 21:23)? How will this affect atmospheric conditions (see Revelation 21:1, 25)?
6. In New Jerusalem, there will be no night or need for sleep (Revelation 21:25). What is the symbolism behind this lack of darkness (see John 8:12; 1 Thessalonians 5:4-8; 1 John 1:5, 7) and weariness (see Isaiah 40:28-31; Galatians 6:9; Revelation 2:3)?

7. The new world will have no more sea (Revelation 21:1). In the Bible, what do seas generally represent (See Psalm 65:5-7; Jonah 2:3; Matthew 14:25-33), and what does their absence reveal about New Jerusalem?
8. New Jerusalem has 12 gates and 12 foundations; how do they demonstrate God's commitment to His people (see Hosea 2:23; Revelation 21:12-14)?
9. What is notable about the gold that makes up New Jerusalem (see Revelation 21:18, 21), and what reality does this symbolize (see Psalm 139:1-12; Jeremiah 23:24)?
10. Why does New Jerusalem have no temple (see Revelation 21:22, 22:4)? How are we to behave as the temple of God as we wait for Christ's return (see 1 Corinthians 3:16-17; 6:12-20; Ephesians 2:19-22)?

Important Takeaways for Us Today

1. Consider how we ought to live in response to God's greatness as described in Colossians 1:16-17:
   a. All things were created by God
   b. All things were created through God
   c. All things were created for God
   d. All things consist in God
   e. God is before all things
2. Revelation 21:23 speaks of God's glory lighting New Jerusalem, but even now God's glory can light up our hearts. How has the light of the Lord illuminated your path (see 2 Corinthians 3:17-18)?

22

A Glimpse into Eternity

REVELATION 22

We live in a sick world. We are surrounded by indiscriminate death, corruption in high places, economic turmoil, and natural disasters—but this is only a blip considering eternity. One day there will be no more curse, but rather, the healing of the nations and the restoration of what was lost in the fall of man. What a great hope we have as believers! Let us be blessed with "he who keeps the words of the prophecy of this book" (Revelation 22:7) and "those who do His commandments, that they may have the right to the tree of life, and may enter through the gates into the city" (Revelation 22:14). Come, Lord Jesus!

New Jerusalem Geography

Frequent Phrases

The last chapter of Revelation has three oft-repeated phrases: "water of life," "tree of life," and "I am coming quickly."

River of Life

The river, or fountain, of life is mentioned three times in Revelation:

> **Revelation 21:6b**—"I will give of the fountain of the water of life freely to him who thirsts."

> **REVELATION 22:1**–"He showed me a pure river of water of life, clear as crystal, proceeding from the throne of God and of the Lamb."
>
> **REVELATION 22:17**–"The Spirit and the bride say, 'Come!' And let him who hears say, 'Come!' And let him who thirsts come. Whoever desires, let him take the water of life freely."

And as Revelation 22:1 says, this river flows from God's throne. Remember, the streets will not be asphalt, but gold like glass, though our imagination strains to conceptualize this.

> **1 Corinthians 2:9**—"As it is written: 'Eye has not seen, nor ear heard, nor have entered into the heart of man the things which God has prepared for those who love Him.'"

Tree of Life

The tree of life is mentioned three times in Revelation.

> **Revelation 2:7b**—"To him who overcomes I will give to eat from the tree of life, which is in the midst of the Paradise of God."

> **REVELATION 22:2a**–"In the middle of its street, and on either side of the river, was the tree of life."

REVELATION 22:14–"Blessed are those who do His commandments, that they may have the right to the tree of life, and may enter through the gates into the city."

This tree is first mentioned in Genesis.

> **Genesis 2:9**—"Out of the ground the LORD God made every tree grow that is pleasant to the sight and good for food. The tree of life was also in the midst of the garden, and the tree of the knowledge of good and evil."

God planted the tree of life alongside the tree of the knowledge of good and evil, putting the choice of whether to choose God or to choose sin side by side. God gave mankind a choice so that a relationship with Him could be based on a love that is freely chosen. Unfortunately, man chose to sin. Eve was deceived, Adam condoned her sin, and mankind fell in one day. This wrong decision removed the tree of life from mankind.

> **Genesis 3:22-24**—"The LORD God said, 'Behold, the man has become like one of Us, to know good and evil. And now, lest he put out his hand and take also of the tree of life, and eat, and live forever'—therefore the LORD God sent him out of the garden of Eden to till the ground from which he was taken. So He drove out the man; and He placed cherubim at the east of the garden of Eden, and a flaming sword which turned every way, to guard the way to the tree of life."

This was for man's own good, to prevent Adam and Eve from eating from the tree of life and sealing their sinful states eternally. God, in His mercy, thought of paving the way for man's redemption even then.

When the worldwide flood occurred, God must have supernaturally plucked up the tree of life from the earth and kept it for this future moment. And in New Jerusalem, all the saints will be able to eat from this tree, having been already sealed in their reconciled states.

Each Tree

Is there one tree of life or are there several trees of life?

> **REVELATION 22:2b**–"…the tree of life, which bore twelve fruits, each tree yielding its fruit every month. The leaves of the tree were for the healing of the nations."

People debate whether the tree of life is one tree or multiple trees because it is difficult to determine this from the language in the biblical text. In Genesis, there is one tree; but in Revelation, some scholars believe there is more than one because of the phrase "each tree." Other scholars believe the language simply indicates that the tree is large and overwhelming enough that its branches drape over both sides of the river, thus taking up the space of multiple trees.

Probably the better interpretation is that there are multiple trees of the same kind as the tree of life.

And though our glorified bodies will not need food to maintain themselves, we will be able to eat for pleasure.

Every Month

God is eternal, and thus He is outside the space-time continuum:

> **2 Peter 3:8**—"Beloved, do not forget this one thing, that with the Lord one day is as a thousand years, and a thousand years as one day."

Though the Lord entered our time to live and die for us—that is the gospel—He does not live constrained by time. Despite this, the concept of time will exist in the New Jerusalem, for the tree of life will yield fruit every month. It will simply be a different kind of time—one defined not by aging, but continuance.

Healing of the Nations

The phrase "the healing of the nations" does not signify that people will still get sick during this time, for in the Greek text, "healing" can be translated as "health-giving" rather than "health-restoring."

No More Curse

> **REVELATION 22:3**–"There shall be no more curse, but the throne of God and of the Lamb shall be in it, and His servants shall serve Him."

Jesus has redeemed us from the curse. Remember, after man's disobedience in Genesis 3, God cursed the man, woman, and serpent. He cursed the man with intensive and unproductive labor, the woman with pain in childbirth and friction between the two sexes, and all creation with death.

> **Genesis 2:17**—"Of the tree of the knowledge of good and evil you shall not eat, for in the day that you eat of it you shall surely die."

Jesus broke the curse and promised us eternal life if we come to Him in faith.

> **Galatians 3:10-11**—"For as many as are of the works of the law are under the curse; for it is written, 'Cursed is everyone who does not continue in all things which are written in the book of the law, to do them.' But that no one is justified by the law in the sight of God is evident, for 'the just shall live by faith.'"

> **Galatians 3:13-14**—"Christ has redeemed us from the curse of the law, having become a curse for us (for it is written, 'Cursed is everyone who hangs on a tree'), that the blessing of Abraham might come upon the Gentiles in Christ Jesus, that we might receive the promise of the Spirit through faith."

The curse has no more power over us, for Christ took the curse upon Himself!

Bear His Name

> **REVELATION 22:4**–"They shall see His face, and His name shall be on their foreheads."

There will come a time when we will see our Lord face to face, and we will have some form of mark that forever identifies us with Him, for we belong to Him.

No Night

> **REVELATION 22:5**–"There shall be no night there: They need no lamp nor light of the sun, for the Lord God gives them light. And they shall reign forever and ever."

There will be no more nighttime or sleeping. Our glorified bodies will not need them.

The Time Is Near

Faithful and True

> **REVELATION 22:6**–"He said to me, 'These words are faithful and true.' And the Lord God of the holy prophets sent His angel to show His servants the things which must shortly take place."

The reminder that what John saw and described is true is important because what God showed him is so wondrous that the prophecy is almost hard to believe.

Coming Quickly

> **REVELATION 22:7a**–"Behold, I am coming quickly!"

Jesus again repeated He will come "quickly"—meaning "suddenly" or "unexpectedly," not "soon." This saying is repeated three times, in verses 7, 12, and 20, to emphasize the suddenness of Jesus' appearing.

> **REVELATION 22:12**–"Behold, I am coming quickly, and My reward is with Me, to give to every one according to his work."
>
> **REVELATION 22:20**–"He who testifies to these things says, 'Surely I am coming quickly.' Amen. Even so, come, Lord Jesus!"

Revelation Beatitudes

Jesus said those who keep His Word are "blessed," which is *makarios* in the Greek text, meaning "oh how happy!" And this is one of the seven beatitudes in Revelation—one less than in Jesus' Sermon on the Mount recorded in Matthew 5.

Here are Revelation's seven beatitudes:

1. A blessing on those who read and keep God's Word:

> **Revelation 1:3**—"Blessed is he who reads and those who hear the words of this prophecy, and keep those things which are written in it; for the time is near."

2. A blessing on the tribulation martyrs:

> **Revelation 14:13b**—"Write: 'Blessed are the dead who die in the Lord from now on.'"

3. A blessing on those who clothe themselves in Jesus' purity:

    Revelation 16:15—"Behold, I am coming as a thief. Blessed is he who watches, and keeps his garments, lest he walk naked and they see his shame."

4. A blessing on those who attend Jesus' marriage celebration:

    Revelation 19:9a—"Write: 'Blessed are those who are called to the marriage supper of the Lamb!'"

5. A blessing on those who are a part of the first resurrection:

    Revelation 20:6—"Blessed and holy is he who has part in the first resurrection. Over such the second death has no power, but they shall be priests of God and of Christ, and shall reign with Him a thousand years."

6. A blessing on those who keep God's Word:

    REVELATION 22:7b–"Blessed is he who keeps the words of the prophecy of this book."

7. A blessing on those who obey His commandments:

    REVELATION 22:14–"Blessed are those who do His commandments, that they may have the right to the tree of life, and may enter through the gates into the city."

Worship God

REVELATION 22:8–"Now I, John, saw and heard these things. And when I heard and saw, I fell down to worship before the feet of the angel who showed me these things."

At this point, John impulsively fell at the angel's feet, perhaps out of a need to worship after being overwhelmed by the visions of the New Jerusalem, but the angel corrected him.

> **REVELATION 22:9**–"He said to me, 'See that you do not do that. For I am your fellow servant, and of your brethren the prophets, and of those who keep the words of this book. Worship God.'"

The worship of angels is not of God. It is demonic. Worship belongs to God alone.

Prophecy Not Sealed

> **REVELATION 22:10**–"He said to me, 'Do not seal the words of the prophecy of this book, for the time is at hand.'"

In Daniel 12:4, God told Daniel to seal up the words of the prophecy "until the time of the end." But here, God told John to "not seal" these words, signifying that the time was at hand. If the words were relevant then, they are especially relevant now.

Decisions Permanent

> **REVELATION 22:11**–"He who is unjust, let him be unjust still; he who is filthy, let him be filthy still; he who is righteous, let him be righteous still; he who is holy, let him be holy still."

This sounds odd, but when the angel tells each man that he should remain as he is, he is saying that, by the end of the tribulation and millennium, there will be nothing left that can be done for sinful humanity. God will have done all He could do to warn people and draw them to Himself. But a time will come when everyone will have sealed their final destinations by how they have responded to Jesus. At that point, witnessing to the unsaved will no longer be our responsibility.

Message to the Churches

Our Works

> **REVELATION 22:12**–"Behold, I am coming quickly, and My reward is with Me, to give to every one according to his work."

Note, we are saved according to Christ's finished work on the cross, not according to our works. However, we are rewarded for works done for Him.

God Eternal

> **REVELATION 22:13**–"I am the Alpha and the Omega, the Beginning and the End, the First and the Last."

City Gates

> **REVELATION 22:14**–"Blessed are those who do His commandments, that they may have the right to the tree of life, and may enter through the gates into the city."

There will be no one climbing over the city walls. All people will enter through the gates, or not at all.

> **REVELATION 22:15**–"Outside are dogs and sorcerers and sexually immoral and murderers and idolaters, and whoever loves and practices a lie."

This is not talking about your pets. The word "dog" references the morally impure. The unrighteous will have already been cast out.

Jesus Described

> **REVELATION 22:16**—"I, Jesus, have sent My angel to testify to you these things in the churches. I am the Root and the Offspring of David, the Bright and Morning Star."

This is the only time in the whole Bible we find the emphatic statement "I, Jesus."

Jesus then said He is both the root and the fruit of David. He is the root because He preceded David as the Eternal God, but He is also the fruit of David because He came to Earth born of a virgin and to an adoptive dad, and both parents could trace their lineages to David. Hence, Jesus has the biological and legal right to the throne of David.

Jesus also referred to Himself as the "Bright and Morning Star," the North Star who points the right direction for all things.

An Invitation

> **REVELATION 22:17**—"The Spirit and the bride say, 'Come!' And let him who hears say, 'Come!' And let him who thirsts come. Whoever desires, let him take the water of life freely."

Jesus offers everyone a generous invitation.

A Warning

> **REVELATION 22:18-19**—"I testify to everyone who hears the words of the prophecy of this book: If anyone adds to these things, God will add to him the plagues that are written in this book; and if anyone takes away from the words of the book of this

prophecy, God shall take away his part from the Book of Life, from the holy city, and from the things which are written in this book."

There is a high price to pay for tampering with the Word of God.

If you add to the Bible, that is legalism. If you subtract from the Bible, that is liberalism.

Both forms of tampering exist in our day. Legalists want to impose standards on you that add to what God has to say, making it harder and more burdensome to walk the Christian life. Liberals want to take away standards, selectively choosing what they want from the Bible until they have deboned God's Word and made a god that is palatable to them. Do not fall for either snare.

Come, Lord Jesus

REVELATION 22:20—"He who testifies to these things says, 'Surely I am coming quickly.' Amen. Even so, come, Lord Jesus!"

"Come, Lord Jesus!" in Aramaic is *Maranatha*.

Grace of God

REVELATION 22:21—"The grace of our Lord Jesus Christ be with you all. Amen."

The last sentence of the last book of the Bible is a benediction of grace. Praise God! We can look up, knowing our redemption is near. May we walk worthy, ready for His return.

Reflections on Revelation 22

Getting Started

In Revelation 22:13, Jesus emphasized—three times—His eternity and ability to see time from beginning to end. Why is this emphasis necessary to our understanding of and trust in the contents of this book?

Study Questions

1. Where does the river of life flow from (Revelation 22:1), and what does the source of the water symbolize (see Psalm 51:7; 1 Corinthians 6:11; Revelation 21:6)?
2. When was the tree of life first mentioned (see Genesis 2:9), and why did God, in His mercy, remove it from mankind (see Genesis 3:22-24)? Has God ever removed something from your life out of mercy?
3. Why did God allow the tree of the knowledge of good and evil to exist in His perfect world (see Genesis 2:9)? How does the presence of the tree of life in New Jerusalem emphasize the saints' choices (see John 3:16-18) and their perfected state (see Genesis 3:22-24; Philippians 1:6; Revelation 2:7; 22:14)?
4. How will the concept of time be different in New Jerusalem (see 2 Peter 3:8)? What victory is implied in this new kind of time defined by continuity instead of aging (see John 11:25-26; 1 Corinthians 15:26; Revelation 20:14)?
5. Why would God provide a tree with leaves for "the healing of the nations" (Revelation 22:2) if we have glorified bodies (see 1 Corinthians 15:42-49; Philippians 3:20-21)? What does the word "nations" emphasize about God's people (see Acts 17:24-28; Isaiah 56:3-8; 61:11)?

6. Revelation 22:3 promises that there will be "no more curse" on that day; what is implied in this promise about the condition of the present world? What is the curse Jesus delivered us from (see Galatians 3:10-11, 13-14), and how will that deliverance culminate in the end of time (see Genesis 3:16-19; Romans 8:18-23)?
7. What does the mark on the saints' foreheads represent (see Isaiah 49:16; Revelation 22:4)? How does this mutual belonging affect your understanding of who you are?
8. Why did John end the book of Revelation with the reminder that God's words are faithful and true (Revelation 22:6)? Which part of God's Word seems too amazing to be true, and how does knowing His promises are true minister to you?
9. Three times, Revelation 22 tells us that Jesus will come suddenly—in verses 7, 12, and 20. How does this oft-repeated phrase relate to Jesus' command for John to not seal the prophecy (Revelation 22:10)? How should the unexpected nature of Christ's coming affect how we walk before the Lord (see Matthew 24:42-45; Mark 13:32-37; Revelation 22:12)?
10. What does the phrase "let him be" in Revelation 22:11 signify? How does that add urgency to God's reminder of the separation between those within New Jerusalem and those without (see John 10:7-9; Revelation 22:14-15)? How can we proclaim Jesus' invitation for unbelievers to come to Him while there is still time (see Revelation 22:17)?
11. Revelation 22:14 gives us the final beatitude of Revelation. Who is this final blessing for, and how does it relate to Jesus' warning about tampering with His Word (Revelation 22:18-19)?
12. In Revelation 22:16, as part of His farewell, Jesus gave the emphatic statement, "I, Jesus"—the only one in all of Scripture—and chose to describe Himself as the "Root and Offspring of David." How does this title relate to the promise

of His return in Revelation 22:20 (see Isaiah 9:6; Amos 9:11-15; 2 Thessalonians 2:8)?

Important Takeaways for Us Today

1. Revelation 22 shows us paradise restored—and better than before, for while Genesis 2:9 speaks about one tree of life, Revelation 22:2 speaks of several. How does this reflect God's restorative power (see Ruth 4:14-15; Isaiah 61:6-7; Joel 2:25-26; Romans 5:11-21)?
2. How have you seen God's restorative grace in your life? Revelation 22:1 shows the cleansing river coming from the Lamb's throne, but the Bible tells us we can experience God's cleansing today through belief in Jesus unto salvation (see Revelation 7:13-14). But there is another kind of cleansing that we do day by day (see John 13:3-10). How do you continually cleanse yourself (see 2 Corinthians 7:1; Ephesians 5:26; 1 John 1:7, 9)?

What's Next?

No one knows the full story but the Father, yet we have been gifted this prophecy, this revelation, and told to hear and obey it that we may be blessed and able to "discern the signs of the times" (Matthew 16:3). But Revelation is not the only book that covers the topic of the end of the age.

If you want to continue to learn about the end times,
check out Pastor Gary's Bible studies on Daniel, Ezekiel, and Joel at
cornerstonechapel.net/teachings!

Notes

Chapter 3—Letters to Our Age: Revelation 3

1. Skip Heitzig, *You Can Understand the Book of Revelation* (Eugene, OR: Harvest House, 2011), 46.

Chapter 6—The Beginning of the End: Revelation 6

1. "UN Report: Global hunger numbers rose to as many as 828 million in 2021," *World Health Organization*, July 6, 2022, https://www.who.int/news/item/06-07-2022-un-report—global-hunger-numbers-rose-to-as-many-as-828-million-in-2021.
2. Pat Lee Shipman, "The Bright Side of the Black Death," *American Scientist*, https://www.americanscientist.org/article/the-bright-side-of-the-black-death.
3. Chris Cicaccia, "The moon is 'rusting' and scientists are stunned," *Fox*, September 6, 2020, https://www.foxnews.com/science/moon-rusting-scientists-stunned.

Chapter 7—The Remnant: Revelation 7

1. "How Many Jehovah's Witnesses Are There Worldwide?," *JW.org*, https://www.jw.org/en/jehovahs-witnesses/faq/how-many-jw/.

Chapter 8—The Calm and the Storm: Revelation 8

1. "Space Menace Looms Centuries Away," *CBS News*, April 4, 2002, https://www.cbsnews.com/news/space-menace-looms-centuries-away/.
2. Sarah Sambolich, "Ask-A-Naturalist: Do phytoplankton produce more oxygen than a rainforest? If so, does the oxygen they produce go into the atmosphere or does it just remain dissolved in the ocean?," *Newport Bay Conservancy*, December 1, 2020, https://newportbay.org/ask-a-naturalist-do-phytoplankton-produce-more-oxygen-than-a-rainforest-if-so-does-the-oxygen-they-produce-go-into-the-atmosphere-or-does-it-just-remain-dissolved-in-the-ocean/.
3. Chris Baraniuk, "What it's like to sail a giant ship on Earth's busiest seas," *BBC*, November 28, 2016, https://www.bbc.com/future/article/20161128-what-its-like-to-sail-colossal-ships-on-earths-busiest-sea.
4. Robyn White, "Chernobyl Aftermath: How Long Will Exclusion Zone Be Uninhabitable?," *Newsweek*, October 14, 2022, https://www.newsweek.com/chernobyl-aftermath-how-long-will-exclusion-zone-uninhabitable-1751834#.
5. Serge Schmemann, "The Talk of Moscow: The Chernobyl Fallout: Apocalyptic Tale and Fear," *The New York Times*, July 26, 1986, https://www.nytimes.com/1986/07/26/world/the-talk-of-moscow-chernobyl-fallout-apocalyptic-tale-and-fear.html.

Chapter 9—Out of the Abyss: Revelation 9

1. See James D. Burke, "Moon," *Britannica*, updated February 3, 2025, https://www.britannica.com/place/Moon; and "Core," *National Geographic*, https://education.nationalgeographic.org/resource/core/.

Chapter 12—A Temporary Reign of Terror: Revelation 12

1. The Times of Israel staff, "Full text of Netanyahu 2015 address to the UN General Assembly, *The Times of Israel*, October 1, 2015, https://www.timesofisrael.com/full-text-of-netanyahu-2015-address-to-the-un-general-assembly/.

Chapter 13—The Two Beasts: Revelation 13

1. Ian Johnson, "Who killed more: Hitler, Stalin, or Mao," *MCLC Resource Center*, February 8, 2018, https://u.osu.edu/mclc/2018/02/08/who-killed-more-hitler-stalin-or-mao/.

Chapter 14—Protected from Wrath: Revelation 14

1. This quote is widely attributed to Jan Tinbergen, but the original source of it is unknown.
2. Ben Wolfgang, "Hillary Clinton dreams of 'open borders': leaked speech excerpts," *Washington Times*, October 8, 2016, https://www.washingtontimes.com/news/2016/oct/8/hillary-clinton-dreams-open-borders-leaked-speech-/.
3. Eric H. Cline, *The Battles of Armageddon* (Ann Arbor, MI: University of Michigan, 2002), 142, ellipsis and brackets in original.

Chapter 16—Torment on Earth: Revelation 16

1. Henry M. Morris, *The Revelation Record: A Scientific and Devotional Commentary on the Prophetic Book of the End Times* (Carol Stream, IL: Tyndale House, 1983), 303-304.
2. Katharina Buchholz, "Rising Sea Levels Will Threaten 200 Million People by 2100," *Statista*, https://www.statista.com/chart/19884/number-of-people-affected-by-rising-sea-levels-per-country/.
3. "2023 Report on International Religious Freedom: Ethiopia," *U.S. Department of State*, https://www.state.gov/reports/2023-report-on-international-religious-freedom/ethiopia/.
4. "2016 Report on International Religious Freedom," *U.S. Department of State*, https://www.state.gov/reports/2016-report-on-international-religious-freedom/libya/.

Chapter 17—The Fall of the One-World Religion: Revelation 17

1. "Washington Monument," *National Park Service*, https://www.nps.gov/wamo/learn/historyculture/index.htm.

Chapter 18— The Fall of the One-World Government: Revelation 18

1. Joshua Becker, "21 Surprising Statistics That Reveal How Much Stuff We Actually Own," *becoming minimalist*, https://www.becomingminimalist.com/clutter-stats/.

Chapter 20—The Prince of Peace: Revelation 20

1. Tara Isabella Burton, "Pope Francis reportedly denies the existence of hell. Vatican panics," *Vox*, March 30, 2018, https://www.vox.com/2018/3/30/17179952/pope-francis-hell-vatican-interview-scalfari-italian.
2. Patrick Buchanan, "Does Pope Francis Believe in Hell?," *Newsmax*, March 30, 2018, https://www.newsmax.com/patrickbuchanan/pope-church-vatican-catholic/2018/03/29/id/851585/.

Chapter 21—A New Beginning: Revelation 21

1. Henry M. Morris, *The Revelation Record* (Wheaton, IL: Tyndale, 1983), 451.